Listening & Speaking **1**

Cheryl Benz

Kara Dworak

HEINLE
CENGAGE Learning™

Australia · Brazil · Japan · Korea · Mexico · Singapore · Spain · United Kingdom · United States

HEINLE
CENGAGE Learning™

Listening and Speaking 1
Cheryl Benz, Kara Dworak

Development Editors: Jennifer Monaghan, Jill Korey O'Sullivan

Sr. Production Coordinator: Maryellen E. Killeen

Market Development Director: Charlotte Sturdy

Sr. Manufacturing Coordinator: Mary Beth Hennebury

Interior Design: Julia Gecha

Illustrations: Pre-Press Company, Inc., Anthony Accardo

Photo Researcher: Martha Friedman

Cover Designer: Ha Nguyen Design

Cover Image: PhotoDisc®

Compositor: Pre-Press Company, Inc.

Freelance Production Editor: Janet McCartney

Copy Editor: Donald Pharr

Printer: Transcontinental

Library of Congress Number:

ISBN-13: 978-0-8384-0009-8

ISBN-10: 0-8384-0009-4

Heinle
25 Thomson Place
Boston, MA 02210
USA

Cengage Learning is a leading provider of customized learning solutions with office locations around the globe, including Singapore, the United Kingdom, Australia, Mexico, Brazil and Japan. Locate our local office at: **international.cengage.com/region**

Cengage Learning products are represented in Canada by Nelson Education, Ltd.

Visit Heinle online at **elt.heinle.com**
Visit our corporate website at **cengage.com**

Sevana

萨娃娜

Printed in Canada
10   11 10 09 08

A VERY SPECIAL THANK YOU

The publisher and authors would like to thank the following coordinators and instructors who have offered many helpful insights and suggestions for change throughout the development of the new *Tapestry*.

Alicia Aguirre, *Cañada College*
Fred Allen, *Mission College*
Maya Alvarez-Galvan, *University of Southern California*
Geraldine Arbach, *Collège de l'Outaouais, Canada*
Dolores Avila, *Pasadena City College*
Sarah Bain, *Eastern Washington University*
Kate Baldus, *San Francisco State University*
Fe Baran, *Chabot College*
Gail Barta, *West Valley College*
Karen Bauman, *Biola University*
Liza Becker, *Mt. San Antonio College*
Leslie Biaggi, *Miami-Dade Community College*
Andrzej Bojarczak, *Pasadena City College*
Nancy Boyer, *Golden West College*
Glenda Bro, *Mt. San Antonio College*
Brooke Brummitt, *Palomar College*
Linda Caputo, *California State University, Fresno*
Alyce Campbell, *Mt. San Antonio College*
Barbara Campbell, *State University of New York, Buffalo*
Robin Carlson, *Cañada College*
Ellen Clegg, *Chapman College*
Karin Cintron, *Aspect ILS*
Diane Colvin, *Orange Coast College*
Martha Compton, *University of California, Irvine*
Nora Dawkins, *Miami-Dade Community College*
Beth Erickson, *University of California, Davis*
Charles Estus, *Eastern Michigan University*
Gail Feinstein Forman, *San Diego City College*
Jeffra Flaitz, *University of South Florida*
Kathleen Flynn, *Glendale Community College*
Ann Fontanella, *City College of San Francisco*
Sally Gearhart, *Santa Rosa Junior College*
Alice Gosak, *San José City College*
Kristina Grey, *Northern Virginia Community College*
Tammy Guy, *University of Washington*
Gail Hamilton, *Hunter College*
Patty Heiser, *University of Washington*
Virginia Heringer, *Pasadena City College*

Catherine Hirsch, *Mt. San Antonio College*
Helen Huntley, *West Virginia University*
Nina Ito, *California State University, Long Beach*
Patricia Jody, *University of South Florida*
Diana Jones, *Angloamericano, Mexico*
Loretta Joseph, *Irvine Valley College*
Christine Kawamura, *California State University, Long Beach*
Gregory Keech, *City College of San Francisco*
Kathleen Keesler, *Orange Coast College*
Daryl Kinney, *Los Angeles City College*
Maria Lerma, *Orange Coast College*
Mary March, *San José State University*
Heather McIntosh, *University of British Columbia, Canada*
Myra Medina, *Miami-Dade Community College*
Elizabeth Mejia, *Washington State University*
Cristi Mitchell, *Miami-Dade Community College*
Sylvette Morin, *Orange Coast College*
Blanca Moss, *El Paso Community College*
Karen O'Neill, *San José State University*
Bjarne Nielsen, *Central Piedmont Community College*
Katy Ordon, *Mission College*
Luis Quesada, *Miami-Dade Community College*
Gustavo Ramírez Toledo, *Colegio Cristóbol Colón, Mexico*
Nuha Salibi, *Orange Coast College*
Alice Savage, *North Harris College*
Dawn Schmid, *California State University, San Marcos*
Mary Kay Seales, *University of Washington*
Denise Selleck, *City College of San Francisco*
Gail Slater, *Brooklyn and Staten Island Superintendency*
Susanne Spangler, *East Los Angeles College*
Karen Stanley, *Central Piedmont Community College*
Sara Storm, *Orange Coast College*
Margaret Teske, *ELS Language Centers*
Maria Vargas-O'Neel, *Miami-Dade Community College*
James Wilson, *Mt. San Antonio College and Pasadena City College*
Karen Yoshihara, *Foothill College*

ACKNOWLEDGMENTS

I'm profoundly grateful for the unconditional support and encouragement offered to me during this project. In particular, I wish to thank my editors, Erik Gundersen, Jennifer Monaghan, Susana Christie, and Jill Kinkade; all the *Tapestry* authors, especially Mary Gill, Virginia Guleff, and Meredith Pike-Baky; my family, Richard and Maureen Dworak, Herman and Marion Dworak, Rebecca and Joe Davies; my friends, Carol McQuirk, Julaine Herreid, Stefan Rosner, Stephanie Basso, Lisa Evans, Tony Albert, Leslie Kelly, Karen Poremski, and the Dahlquists; every one of my colleagues at San Jose State University, but especially Marianne Walker and Karen O'Neill; my mentors and friends, Doug Brown, Kathy Sherak, and Jennifer Schmidt; West Valley Community College, in particular Gail Barta and Carl Jones; and most especially, the inspiring students I have had the opportunity to learn from over the years. Thank you all so much. —K. D.

Tapestry Listening & Speaking 1: Contents

CHAPTER	LISTENING & SPEAKING SKILLS FOCUS	LANGUAGE LEARNING STRATEGIES
1 Meetings and Greetings Page 2	Introducing yourself and others in both formal and informal ways Practicing speaking English with classmates Using appropriate body language when meeting and greeting people Greeting people in both formal and informal ways	Practice speaking English with classmates as often as possible. Make connections between new things and familiar words and ideas.
2 Finding Your Way Page 26	Understanding and giving directions Using prepositions of direction Asking for clarification when you don't understand someone Learning how to pronounce new words	Use movement to learn new expressions that you hear. Learn how new words are pronounced.
3 A Full Life Page 52	Talking about your regular schedule Asking questions and participating in class Using adverbs of frequency Listening for the topic of conversations Starting conversations with new people	Ask questions and participate in class in order to learn English. Listen for the topic or subject of a conversation.
4 It's Raining Cats and Dogs Page 78	Talking about the weather Asking questions about the weather Using a graphic organizer to understand and remember what you hear Participating in a group presentation	Use mental pictures to remember new words. Use a graphic organizer to understand and remember what you hear.
5 To Your Health Page 106	Describing symptoms Understanding and giving advice Knowing when to give strong advice and when to make suggestions Making an appointment on the telephone	Practice telephone conversations before you call. Listen for sequence words and phrases to help you understand what you hear.

ACADEMIC POWER STRATEGIES	CNN VIDEO CLIPS	PRONUNCIATION: THE SOUND OF IT	LISTENING OPPORTUNITIES
Learn how to address your teachers.	"Empty Nest" Parents bring their children to college for their freshman year.	Reductions	Listening 1: five conversations between people who are meeting each other for the first time Listening 2: four more conversations of people meeting, this time with problems in the formality level of their speech Listening 3: six conversations of people greeting each other
Get to know campus resources.	"The Sparrow" An introduction to a new type of transportation.	Syllable stress	Listening 1: a recording of directions to West Valley Community College in Saratoga, California Listening 2: a conversation between two students in which one student gives campus directions to the other Listening 3: three students give directions to places on campus
Join a club or group on campus.	"Going Back to School" A mother with kids in school goes back to college.	Sentence stress	Listening 1: two students talk about their schedules Listening 2: a conversation between a "morning person" and a "night owl" Listening 3: an automated phone service which gives information about what films are currently playing in the area Listening 4: four conversations involving small talk
Learn to work and study well with other students.	"Global Warming" Politicians and scientists talk about the causes of global warming.	Pronouncing the /ng/ sound	Listening 1: four conversations about the weather Listening 2: a weather report
Find healthy ways to reduce stress in order to help you study more effectively.	"Snacking" A look at the snacks Americans love to eat.	Pronouncing the /th/ sound	Listening 1: six conversations in which people describe their symptoms Listening 2: a student gets health advice from his friend, from his mother, and from his doctor Listening 3: a woman makes a doctor's appointment over the telephone Listening 4: a student visits a doctor, describes her symptoms, and gets advice on how to stay healthy Listening 5: a lecture on the most frequent excuses people give for not exercising Listening 6: a lecture about staying healthy

CHAPTER	LISTENING & SPEAKING SKILLS FOCUS	LANGUAGE LEARNING STRATEGIES
6 A Human Rainbow Page 132	Describing people and things Talking about similarities and differences in several different ways Using word games to practice English Using analogies to describe complex ideas	Invent a title to summarize what you hear or read. Use word games to practice English.
7 My Hero Page 158	Using a chart to take notes when you listen Describing people's personalities Using adjectives to describe Elaborating on your answers Using music to learn English and improve your pronunciation	Use a chart to help you take good notes when you listen. Use music to help you learn English and improve your pronunciation.
8 Get a Job! Page 182	Focusing on content words to improve your understanding when you listen Talking about habits and routines Asking questions in English Giving formal and informal answers to questions	Focus on content words to improve your understanding when you listen. Use tongue twisters to practice difficult sounds.
9 All in the Family Page 212	Asking about and giving information about families Predicting what you will hear Using time expressions to tell a story Talking about responsibilities Repeating new words and phrases several times	Predict what you will hear before you listen. Repeat new words and phrases several times.
10 The Future Is Now Page 232	Retelling what you hear to someone else Making predictions about the future Talking about plans for the future Changing the tone of your voice when asking different kinds of questions	Repeat or retell what you hear to someone else in order to make sure you understand what you have heard. Use pictures and photos to help you guess the main idea before you listen.

ACADEMIC POWER STRATEGIES	CNN VIDEO CLIPS	PRONUNCIATION: THE SOUND OF IT	LISTENING OPPORTUNITIES
Preview visuals in textbooks to help you prepare for classes.	"Immigrant Professionals" Immigrants talk about adjusting to the demands of the American job market.	Pronouncing the /er/ sound	Listening 1: a listening about the similarities between two friends Listening 2: a lecture about immigration in the United States
Find a mentor who can help you be successful in school.	"Super Barrio!" He's not a typical super hero; Super Barrio helps the poor people of Mexico.	Pronouncing the long e sound	Listening 1: descriptions of seven famous people who many people consider to be "heroes" Listening 2: a listening about the comic book hero Superman Listening 3: three people discuss their personal heroes
Make a career plan to help you prepare for the future.	"Tech Worker Shortage" A tech worker job fair shows that there are many jobs for people with education in technology.	Three different ways to pronounce s	Listening 1: a description of three people's jobs Listening 2: a lecture about career planning
Make a schedule to use your time well.	"Looking for Love" The ways people are looking for love in the '90s.	Pronouncing the simple past /-ed/ sound	Listening 1: two people are interviewed about their families Listening 2: two people are interviewed about their pets Listening 3: a lecture about pet ownership in the United States and Canada Listening 4: four people tell the stories of how they met their partners
Reward yourself for reaching your goals.	"Smart House" A look at the house of the future, which has many advantages, but also has one big problem.	Question intonation	Listening: a listening about toys of the future

Welcome to TAPESTRY!

Empower your students with the **Tapestry Listening & Speaking** series!

Language learning can be seen as an ever-developing tapestry woven with many threads and colors. The elements of the tapestry are related to different language skills such as listening and speaking, reading, and writing; the characteristics of the teachers; the desires, needs, and backgrounds of the students; and the general second language development process. When all of these elements are working together harmoniously, the result is a colorful, continuously growing tapestry of language competence of which the student and the teacher can be proud.

Tapestry is built upon a framework of concepts that helps students become proficient in English and prepared for the academic and social challenges in college and beyond. The following principles underlie the instruction provided in all of the components of the **Tapestry** program:

◆ Empowering students to be responsible for their learning

◆ Using Language Learning Strategies and Academic Power Strategies to enhance one's learning, both in and out of the classroom

◆ Offering motivating activities that recognize a variety of learning styles

◆ Providing authentic and meaningful input to heighten learning and communication

◆ Learning to understand and value different cultures

◆ Integrating language skills to increase communicative competence

◆ Providing goals and ongoing self-assessment to monitor progress

Guide to **Tapestry Listening & Speaking**

Setting Goals focuses students' attention on the learning they will do in each chapter.

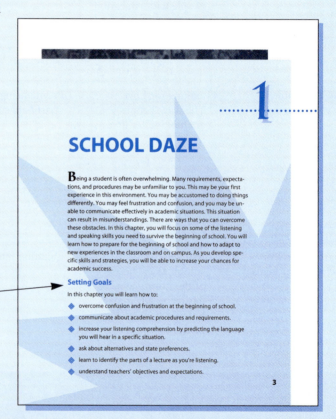

1

SCHOOL DAZE

Being a student is often overwhelming. Many requirements, expectations, and procedures may be unfamiliar to you. This may be your first experience in this environment. You may be accustomed to doing things differently. You may feel frustration and confusion, and you may be unable to communicate effectively in academic situations. This situation can result in misunderstandings. There are ways that you can overcome these obstacles. In this chapter, you will focus on some of the listening and speaking skills you need to survive the beginning of school. You will learn how to prepare for the beginning of school and how to adapt to new experiences in the classroom and on campus. As you develop specific skills and strategies, you will be able to increase your chances for academic success.

Setting Goals

In this chapter you will learn how to:

◆ overcome confusion and frustration at the beginning of school.

◆ communicate about academic procedures and requirements.

◆ increase your listening comprehension by predicting the language you will hear in a specific situation.

◆ ask about alternatives and state preferences.

◆ learn to identify the parts of a lecture as you're listening.

◆ understand teachers' objectives and expectations.

3

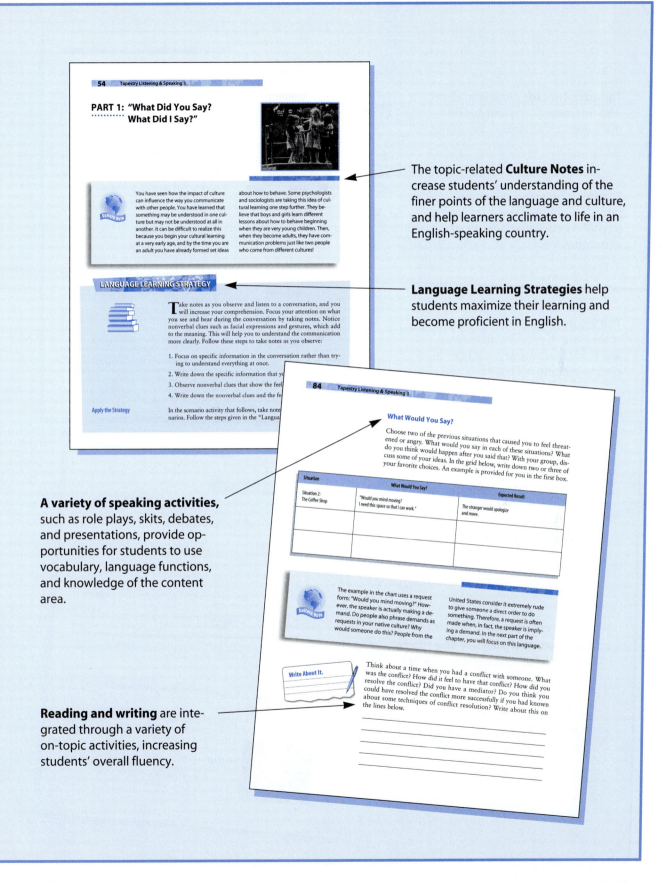

PART 1: "What Did You Say? What Did I Say?"

Culture Note

You have seen how the impact of culture can influence the way you communicate with other people. You have learned that something may be understood in one culture but may not be understood at all in another. It can be difficult to realize this because you begin your cultural learning at a very early age, and by the time you are an adult you have already formed set ideas about how to behave. Some psychologists and sociologists are taking this idea of cultural learning one step further. They believe that boys and girls learn different lessons about how to behave beginning when they are very young children. Then, when they become adults, they have communication problems just like two people who come from different cultures!

LANGUAGE LEARNING STRATEGY

Take notes as you observe and listen to a conversation, and you will increase your comprehension. Focus your attention on what you see and hear during the conversation by taking notes. Notice nonverbal clues such as facial expressions and gestures, which add to the meaning. This will help you to understand the communication more clearly. Follow these steps to take notes as you observe:

1. Focus on specific information in the conversation rather than trying to understand everything at once.
2. Write down the specific information that y...
3. Observe nonverbal clues that show the feel...
4. Write down the nonverbal clues and the fe...

Apply the Strategy   In the scenario activity that follows, take note... narios. Follow the steps given in the "Langua...

The topic-related **Culture Notes** increase students' understanding of the finer points of the language and culture, and help learners acclimate to life in an English-speaking country.

Language Learning Strategies help students maximize their learning and become proficient in English.

What Would You Say?

Choose two of the previous situations that caused you to feel threatened or angry. What would you say in each of these situations? What do you think would happen after you said that? With your group, discuss some of your ideas. In the grid below, write down two or three of your favorite choices. An example is provided for you in the first box.

Situation	What Would You Say?		Expected Result
Situation 2: The Coffee Shop	"Would you mind moving? I need this space so that I can work."		The stranger would apologize and move.

Culture Note

The example in the chart uses a request form: "Would you mind moving?" However, the speaker is actually making a demand. Do people also phrase demands as requests in your native culture? Why would someone do this? People from the United States consider it extremely rude to give someone a direct order to do something. Therefore, a request is often made when, in fact, the speaker is implying a demand. In the next part of the chapter, you will focus on this language.

Write About It.

Think about a time when you had a conflict with someone. What was the conflict? How did it feel to have that conflict? How did you resolve the conflict? Did you have a mediator? Do you think you could have resolved the conflict more successfully if you had known about some techniques of conflict resolution? Write about this on the lines below.

A variety of speaking activities, such as role plays, skits, debates, and presentations, provide opportunities for students to use vocabulary, language functions, and knowledge of the content area.

Reading and writing are integrated through a variety of on-topic activities, increasing students' overall fluency.

Tapestry Threads provide students with interesting facts and quotes that jumpstart classroom discussions.

Engaging listening selections provide authentic news broadcasts, interviews, conversations, debates, and stories.

The Sound of It refines listening, speaking, and pronunciation skills, and helps students gain confidence communicating in English.

REAL PEOPLE/REAL VOICES

Getting Ready to Listen

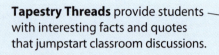

The world is so fast that there are days when the person who says it can't be done is interrupted by the person who is doing it.
—ANONYMOUS

You are going to hear two people talking about the stress in their lives. Andrew is a student who has just finished his first semester at college. Henry is a working man with children. For each of them, make one prediction about what causes them stress. Write down your prediction on the line.

Andrew—college student

I think _____ causes Andrew stress.

Henry—working parent

I think _____ causes Henry stress.

Listen

Listening 1: Andrew's and Henry's Experiences

Write A if the statement is true about Andrew and H if the statement is true about Henry.

1. _____ Worries give him the most stress.
2. _____ He has a frantic schedule.
3. _____ Academic pressure makes him nervous.
4. _____ He worries about his kids.
5. _____ Sport helps him to deal with stress.
6. _____ Solving one problem at a time helps him to deal with stress.

After You Listen

For each of the two speakers you heard on the tape, give a suggestion for how he can deal with his stress.

Andrew: _____

Henry: _____

The Sound of It: "Filler" Sounds and Words

In spoken language, a *filler* is a sound or word that fills in the space and gives the speaker time to think before continuing. In spoken English, "um" is the most common filler. It's important to recognize this sound so that you don't confuse it with part of another word. Listen to the tape again, and count the number of times each speaker uses the filler "um."

Andrew: _____

Henry: _____

Academic Power Strategies give students the knowledge and skills to become successful, independent learners.

Apply the Strategy activities encourage students to take charge of their learning and use their new skills and strategies.

CNN® video clips provide authentic input and further develop listening and speaking skills.

ACADEMIC POWER STRATEGY

Contribute your ideas in group activities. Actively participating in group activities helps you remember your ideas and gives your teacher a chance to see you working hard to succeed in class. There are some easy things you can do to practice speaking in group discussions:

1. Ask questions. Ask your teacher. Ask other students. Show that you are interested and want to learn.
2. Use your notes to help prepare ideas you can share.
3. Paraphrase—repeat in your own words an idea from a lecture, discussion, or activity.
4. If you have something to say but it's not a good time, make a note to yourself and save your good idea to share later in the discussion.

Apply the Strategy

In small groups, discuss your observation of each simulation based on your notes in the grid. Be sure that everyone in the group contributes ideas. Compare your responses to other members of your group. Do you agree or disagree on the problem, the reason, and the perception?

TUNING IN: "The Bilingual Storyteller"

You will see a CNN video clip about a man who tries to help children be proud of their cultural identities. Before you watch the clip, talk with a partner and answer these questions.

Do you think it is easier for children or adults to adapt to a culture that is different from the culture of their families?

Why do you think this?

What are some of the things parents and other adults can do to help children become comfortable in a new culture?

Antonio is a teacher. He tells stories to children. He tells the stories in a mix of English and Spanish. The stories help the children

© CNN

Test-Taking Tips offer students practical steps for improving their test results.

Check Your Progress helps students monitor their own progress.

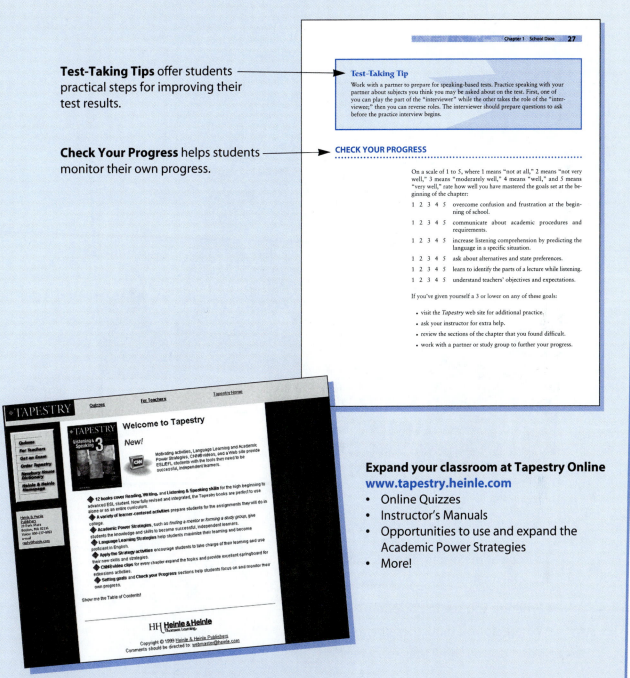

Test-Taking Tip

Work with a partner to prepare for speaking-based tests. Practice speaking with your partner about subjects you think you may be asked about on the test. First, one of you can play the part of the "interviewer" while the other takes the role of the "interviewee;" then you can reverse roles. The interviewer should prepare questions to ask before the practice interview begins.

CHECK YOUR PROGRESS

On a scale of 1 to 5, where 1 means "not at all," 2 means "not very well," 3 means "moderately well," 4 means "well," and 5 means "very well," rate how well you have mastered the goals set at the beginning of the chapter:

1 2 3 4 5 overcome confusion and frustration at the beginning of school.

1 2 3 4 5 communicate about academic procedures and requirements.

1 2 3 4 5 increase listening comprehension by predicting the language in a specific situation.

1 2 3 4 5 ask about alternatives and state preferences.

1 2 3 4 5 learn to identify the parts of a lecture while listening.

1 2 3 4 5 understand teachers' objectives and expectations.

If you've given yourself a 3 or lower on any of these goals:

- visit the *Tapestry* web site for additional practice.
- ask your instructor for extra help.
- review the sections of the chapter that you found difficult.
- work with a partner or study group to further your progress.

Expand your classroom at Tapestry Online
www.tapestry.heinle.com
- Online Quizzes
- Instructor's Manuals
- Opportunities to use and expand the Academic Power Strategies
- More!

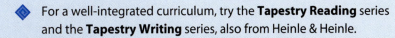

For a well-integrated curriculum, try the **Tapestry Reading** series and the **Tapestry Writing** series, also from Heinle & Heinle.

To learn more about the **Tapestry** principles, read *The Tapestry of Language Learning,* by Rebecca L. Oxford and Robin C. Scarcella, also from Heinle & Heinle Publishers. ISBN 0-8384-2359-0.

Look at the photo. Then discuss these questions with your classmates:

- What do you see in this photo?
- Where do you think these people are?
- What do you think they're saying?

MEETINGS AND GREETINGS

This chapter will help you to meet, greet, and get to know new people in your classes and in your daily life. It will also help you to use the right language for the right situation. What you learn in this chapter will help you right now in your classes. It will also help in the future as you use English for your education, work, and life.

Setting Goals

In this chapter you will learn to:

- introduce yourself and others in both formal and informal ways.

- practice speaking English with classmates.

- use appropriate body language when meeting and greeting people.

- make connections between new things and familiar words and ideas.

- greet people in both formal and informal ways.

- understand and pronounce reductions correctly.

- address your teachers appropriately.

◆ **Getting Started**

What do you already know about introducing yourself and others in English? Work with a few classmates. Answer these questions together:

1. What do people *say* when they introduce themselves? Make a list.

2. What do people *do* when they introduce themselves? Show each other.

3. Share your answers with the class. Your teacher might make a list on the board.

PART 1: Meeting New People

In the United States and Canada, people usually use *formal* language in official situations. It is used in business and between people of different ages. For example, a younger person speaking to an older person should use formal language. On the other hand, *informal* language is usually used in casual situations. Informal language is used in social situations and among people of the same age group. Young people, family members, and good friends usually use informal language with each other.

◆ **Formal or Informal Language?**

Look at the following situations. Should you use formal or informal language? Write *F* for formal. Write *I* for informal.

____F____ speaking with a boss or manager at work

____I____ talking to your brothers and sisters

____F____ talking to your teacher for the first time

____F____ speaking to an older adult

____I____ speaking to classmates

____F____ meeting someone for the first time

◆ **Getting Ready to Listen**

You will hear five introductions. Before you listen, look at the pictures on the following page. Do you think the introduction will be formal or informal? Write *F* for formal or *I* for informal under each picture.

◆ **Listen**

Listening 1: Formal and Informal Introductions

Now listen to the introductions. Is the introduction formal or informal? Check your guesses.

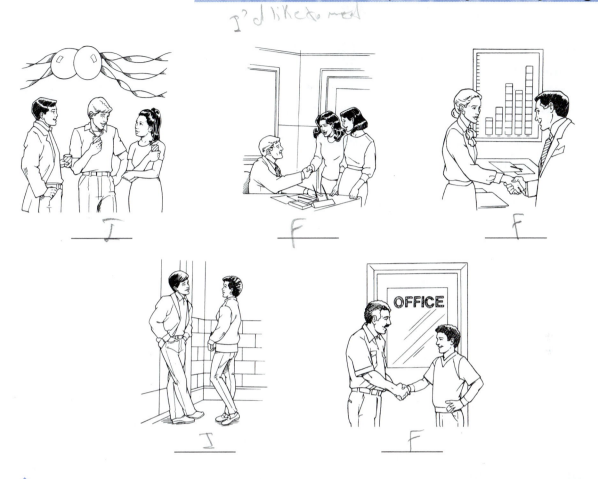

I'd like to med

_I_   _F_   _F_

_I_   _F_

After You Listen

Work with a partner. Why did you think the introductions and pictures were formal or informal? Explain your choices to your partner.

LANGUAGE YOU CAN USE:
INTRODUCING YOURSELF AND OTHERS

Here are some expressions for introducing yourself and introducing others in formal and informal ways:

INTRODUCING YOURSELF	
Formal	**Informal**
Hello. My name is _Sevana_.	Hi. I'm _Sevana_.
I don't think we've met. I'm _??_.	Hi my name's _??_.
_____	_____
_____	_____

> I sometimes think I was born to live up to my name. How could I be anything else but what I am having been named Madonna? I would either have ended up a nun or this.
>
> —MADONNA

INTRODUCING OTHERS	
Formal	**Informal**
I'd like you to meet _Peter_.	This is _____.
I'd like to introduce _Mary_ to you.	This is my friend _____.
_____	_____
_____	_____

USING NEW LANGUAGE

Go back to the list you made in the Getting Started activity.

1. Which introductions are formal? Which are informal?

2. Write each introduction in the correct place on the chart above and on page 5.

3. Practice saying each introduction.

Getting Ready to Listen

Check all the statements that are true.

I know that someone is speaking formally or informally because of

_____ the tone of the person's voice.

_____ the speed of the person's voice.

_____ the words the person uses.

Listen

Listening 2: Formal and Informal Dialogues

You will hear four dialogues. In each dialogue, one person is not speaking appropriately. He or she is speaking too formally or is speaking too informally. Put a check mark in front of the speaker who is not speaking appropriately.

AT A PARTY

___I___	Mark:	Hey, George! This is Sal, my brother.
it's nice to meet you. ___F___	George:	✗ It is certainly a pleasure to meet you, Sal.
___I___	Sal:	Nice to meet you, _too_

> A good name, like good will, is got by many actions and lost by one.
>
> —LORD JEFFERY

IN THE CLASSROOM

_F_	Mr. Macy:	I'm Mr. John Macy, your grammar teacher.
_I_	Mike:	✗ Yo, what's up, Teach?

it's a pleasure to meet you.

IN THE CAFETERIA

_F_	Stephanie:	*Hi* Hello, Victor. I'd like you to meet a new classmate. This is Karen.
_I_	Victor:	Hey, Karen. Nice to meet you.
	Karen:	Nice to meet you.

AT HOME

_F_	Paul:	Patrick, this is my mother, Mrs. Doris Bluefield.
_I_	Patrick:	*Hello,* Hey, Doris. How's it goin'?
_F_	Mrs. Bluefield:	Welcome to our home, Patrick.

Hello Mrs. B. - How are you

After You Listen

Work with a partner.

1. Look again at the dialogues above.

2. Discuss the inappropriate remarks. Were they too formal or too informal? Why?

3. Rewrite the dialogues so that they are all appropriate.

4. Practice the dialogues together.

LANGUAGE LEARNING STRATEGY

Apply the Strategy

Practice speaking English with classmates as often as possible. It helps you to learn to speak and communicate better. Your classmates are good conversation partners. You can practice new things together in class. You can also practice together outside of class. Remember, practice makes perfect.

Right now you are learning different ways to introduce yourself. Practicing introductions now will help you make them in the future. Work with a partner. Practice introducing yourself. Use these situations. Then switch roles and practice again.

(continued on next page)

1. You are in a classroom the first day of class. Another student comes in.

2. You are a professor. A new student comes into your office to meet you.

3. You are at a friend's party. You see a new person standing near you.

4. You are in an office. A new co-worker enters.

BODY LANGUAGE: SHAKING HANDS

palm

People in the United States and Canada often shake hands when they meet each other. This handshake is not the same as the handshake in other countries. Here is how to shake hands appropriately:

- Hold the other person's hand firmly.
- The palm of your hand should cover the palm of the hand of the person you are shaking hands with, not just the fingertips.
- Look the person in the eye and smile when you shake hands.

Practice introducing yourself and shaking hands.

1. Your teacher will give you a situation.

2. Walk around the classroom.

3. Shake hands and introduce yourself according to the situation.

4. Your teacher will say "stop!" and will give you a new situation.

5. Shake hands and introduce yourself according to the new situation.

6. Try to shake hands with as many students as possible.

crashing a party

In classrooms in the United States and Canada, students often talk to each other, not just to the teacher. It is important to know the names of your classmates so you can ask them questions, tell them your ideas, and work together.

LANGUAGE LEARNING STRATEGY

Make connections between new things and familiar words and ideas. Then you can remember more easily. This strategy can help you remember new vocabulary, new names, new places, and new faces. For example, remembering names of new people can be difficult. If you connect a person's name with something familiar, you will remember the name more easily.

Apply the Strategy

To remember new people's names, connect them to familiar words.

1. Think of something that you like that begins with the same letter as your name. Examples:

   Bernd   Ming

   books   music

   Hint: If you cannot think of something, ask your teacher for help.

2. Sit in a circle with your classmates. The first person will say her or his name and what she or he likes. Example:

   "Hello, I'm Bernd. I like books."

3. The second person will say her or his name and what she or he likes _and_ say the first person's name and what she or he likes.

   "My name is Ming. I enjoy music very much. This is Bernd. He likes books."

4. The third person will say her or his name and what she or he likes _and_ say the second person's name and what she or he likes _and_ the first person's name and what she or he likes.

(continued on next page)

"My name is Carol. I like Coca-Cola. This is Ming. She enjoys music. This is Bernd. He likes books."

5. Continue this way until the last person has introduced himself or herself.

6. Now take turns saying every classmate's name.

7. Find out who can say the names most quickly!

FIND SOMEONE WHO . . .

If you want to win friends, make it a point to remember them. If you remember my name, you pay me a subtle compliment; you indicate that I have made an impression on you. Remember my name and you add to my feeling of importance.

—DALE CARNEGIE

It is important to know your classmates. You will work with other students in class. Also, people learn language more easily when they feel more comfortable. This activity will help you to know your classmates.

1. Read the exercise below. If there is anything you do not understand, ask your teacher.

2. Get up and ask classmates questions to find someone who. . . . If they answer "No," say, "OK." Ask another question until someone answers "Yes." Write this person's name after the question.

3. Do not write someone's name more than once.

4. You have ten minutes.

5. Go!

EXAMPLE:

_____ has a pet.

A: Do you have a pet?

B: No.

A: OK. Do you have a car?

B: Yes!

A: Great. How do you spell your name?

B: M-I-G-U-E-L.

A: Thanks, Miguel.

Find someone who . . .

_____ has a pet.

_____ speaks three languages.

_____ has a car.

_____ has four siblings (brothers and sisters).

_____ plays the guitar.

_____ hates fast food.

_____ loves ice cream.

_____ owns a bike.

_____ has a daughter.

_____ is shy.

_____ is married.

_____ has more than 100 books.

_____ has been to more than four countries.

In the United States, people often play games like "Find Someone Who . . . " at parties. These games are called "ice-breakers." They "break the ice" to start conversations between people who don't know each other well.

Why don't we tell each other where we are from?

PART 2: Greeting People You Know

GREETING PEOPLE

There are many ways to say "hello" in English. Make a list of all the ways you know to greet people in English.

1. Hello, how are you?
2. _Hi, what's up?_
3. _yo! what's going on?_
4. _yo! what's up?_
5. _How's it going?_

LANGUAGE YOU CAN USE: GREETING PEOPLE

You learned that introductions can be formal or informal. Greetings can be formal or informal, too. Here are some common greetings.

Hey, how's it going?   Hello, how are you today?
Good morning.   Good evening.
Hi, how are you?   Hi! How're you doing?
Hi, it's nice to see you.   Hello. How have you been?
Good afternoon.   Hey, what's new?

USING NEW LANGUAGE

Work with a partner.

1. Read the greetings above.
2. Write the greetings in the correct box on the next page.
3. Practice saying each greeting.

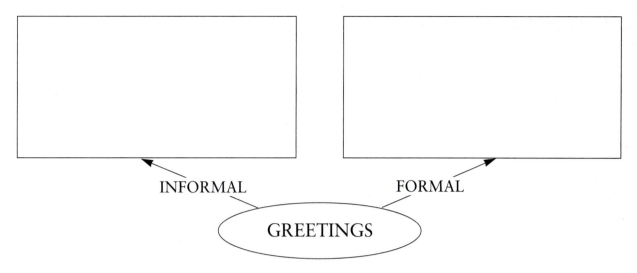

INFORMAL   FORMAL

GREETINGS

Getting Ready to Listen

The rate, or speed, of someone's language can tell you if the person is speaking formally or informally. Discuss these questions with a partner.

1. If someone is speaking formally, does the person speak quickly or slowly?

2. If someone is speaking informally, does the person speak quickly or slowly?

Listen

erbibit - show
they're on exbibition

Listening 3: Listen for Rate of Speech

Listen to the rate of speech in each short conversation. Decide if it is formal or informal.

	Formal	Informal
In a Musuem	✓	
In a Supermarket	✓	
In the Student Union		✓
At a Holiday Dinner		✓
At the Front Door	✓	
In a Professor's Office	✓	

After You Listen

Work with a partner. Listen to the conversations again and discuss these questions:

1. What words tell you whether the conversation is formal or informal?

2. What other clues help you decide?

The Sound of It: Reductions

(reduce sounds)
shorten

rituals - nothing

English speakers do not pronounce all the sounds in every word. This is true especially when they are speaking informally. This is called sound reduction. Look at the examples below.

1. Listen to how they are pronounced by native speakers.

2. Match the complete sentences with the reduced form on the right.

3. Now practice saying the sentences with reductions.

a. How are you doing? _____d_____ /How'r ya?/

b. How is it going? _____e_____ /How'v ya been?/

c. What is happening? _____g_____ /How 'bout you?/

d. How are you? _____f_____ /It's nice ta see ya./

e. How have you been? _____a_____ /How ya doin'?/

f. It's nice to see you. _____b_____ /How'zit goin'?/

g. How about you? _____c_____ /What's happ'nin'?/

Think About It

Speakers of all languages leave out sounds when speaking quickly. Why do you think this happens? Discuss this with a partner.

Culture Note

Most of the time in greetings, when someone asks "How are you?" in English, it just means "Hello." The speaker is not really asking how you feel or how you are doing. If you know someone very well, you may tell the truth about how you feel. You may say "Bad" or "Not so great." But most of the time, everyone says "Fine!"

LANGUAGE YOU CAN USE: RESPONDING TO GREETINGS

It is important to know how to respond to greetings.

GREETINGS	RESPONSES
Hello, how are you?	Fine thanks. What about yourself?
How are you?	Good. And you?
How have you been?	Fine. How have you been?
What's new?	Not much.* What about you?
What's up?	Nothing.* What's up with you?

*Don't say, "Fine" when asked "What's new?" or "What's up?" Say "Nothing" or "Not much."

USING NEW LANGUAGE

1. Work with a partner.

2. Cut a piece of paper into seven equal parts (you can also use seven index cards).

3. On each piece of paper, write one of the complete sentences from The Sound of It.

4. Turn the papers upside down and put them on a table between you and your partner.

5. Take turns choosing a paper.

6. Say the sentence on the paper to your partner in the reduced form.

7. Your partner will answer in an appropriate way. For example:

   A: Chooses a paper with "How are you doing?" on it.
   A: Says: "How ya doin'?"
   B: Says: "Fine, thanks."

 Dialogues

Work with a partner.

1. Write a short dialogue for two people greeting each other.

2. Practice your dialogue.

3. Perform your dialogue for your classmates.

4. Your classmates should guess if your dialogue is formal or informal.

EXAMPLE:

A: Hey, Mike. How's it goin'?

B: Fine. How 'bout you?

A: Not bad.

Informal

In the United States and Canada . . .
Call your teacher by title and last name.
Do not call your teacher by title alone.
Do not call your teacher by title and first name.

Yes:	No:
Mr. Connell	Teacher
Dr. Yee	Doctor Joe
Ms. Rice	Ms. Sylvia

ACADEMIC POWER STRATEGY

Learn how to address your teachers. Every culture addresses teachers differently. For example, in many countries students call all teachers "Teacher." In the United States and Canada, this is not polite. It is important to know your teachers' names and how to address them. Then you can create a good relationship with your teacher. Also, you can ask questions when you need help.

Apply the Strategy

Ask your teachers what they want to be called. Write this information here.

_____

_____

_____

Note: Not every teacher likes to be addressed formally. Teachers will tell you if they prefer a more informal address.

Getting Ready to Read

You are going to read about how people greet each other in different parts of the world. Before you read, answer the following questions with a partner:

1. How do you greet people in your native country? What do you say and do? Show your partner.

2. Are there special rules for children when greeting adults?

Read

Compare Greetings around the World

1 How do you greet your friends when you see them? Do children say "hello" to adults in the same way? There are certain **unwritten rules** for greeting people, which **differ** around the world.

2   In France, for instance, children regularly shake **hands** with one another. A Korean child would **be honored** to shake the hand of an adult, but will more usually bow his or her **head**. Instead of saying "Good morning," both Koreans and Somalis ask "Have you been in peace during the night?" or "Is it peace?"

3   Bowing is something many people around the world do as a form of greeting. In Japan, the bow is usually low, from the **waist.** In Malaysia, Malay people bow only slightly when greeting one another, as well as when passing on the street.

4   Most Hindus use the *namaste* (nah-MAHS-tay) gesture when they greet each other. They place their **palms** together as though in prayer, and nod their heads slightly. Most people also say "Namaste" while gesturing.

◆ **Vocabulary Building**

Look at this vocabulary in the reading. Choose the correct definition below.

1. **Unwritten rules** are

    a. rules that everyone knows but no one talks about.

    b. rules that no one writes.

2. **To differ** means to

    a. argue or fight with someone.

    b. change or be different.

3. **To be honored** means to

    a. to get a special prize.

    b. to feel respected and happy.

Draw a line from the words for different body parts to their correct location on the figure.

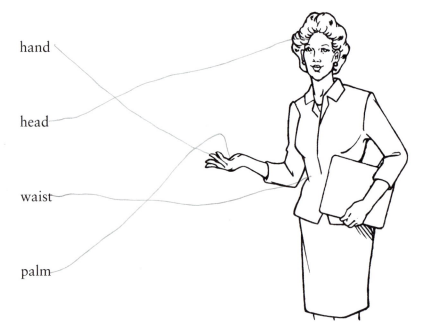

hand

head

waist

palm

◆ **After You Read**

1. Make a small group. If possible, include people from different cultures in your group.

2. Read the following list of situations.

3. Show your group gestures from your native country for those situations.

I don't know.	It's great!
OK.	It's no good.
Stop.	Give it to me.
Good luck.	Goodbye.
Come here.	

THE FAR SIDE   By GARY LARSON

How snakes say goodbye.

Some gestures that are common and acceptable in one culture have a different or negative meaning in another culture. For example, in the United States and Canada the gesture for OK looks like this:

But in Korea that gesture means "money." In Brazil and some other South American countries, that same gesture has a very offensive meaning. That is why it is important to understand the meaning of gestures in different cultures.

◆ Group Activity

The table below describes the different gestures people make in the United States and Canada when they greet each other.

1. Work in a group of three to four students.

2. Read the table below. If you do not understand the gesture, ask your teacher to demonstrate.

3. Show the students in your group how people greet each other in your native country in these situations.

SITUATION

1. Family members meet after being apart for a long time.

2. Business people meet.

3. Neighbors see each other from a distance.

4. Lovers meet.

5. You see a security guard or other service person who works near your home or office.

6. Friends meet.

7. Teenagers meet.

GESTURE

1. They usually hug or put an arm around each other.

2. They shake hands.

3. They wave and say "Hi!"

4. They kiss.

5. Nod your head and smile.

6. They shake hands or nod their head and smile.

7. They slap hands.

1.

2.

3.

4.

5.

6.

7.

left home

TUNING IN: "Empty Nest"

mixed feelings

or

mixed emotions

An *empty nest* is an expression that describes when adult children move out of their parents' house. A nest is a home for birds. When the birds can fly, they leave the nest. Then the nest is empty.

You will watch a video about parents bringing their sons and daughters to college for their freshman year. Before you watch, talk to a classmate about your native culture:

© CNN

1. Do most college students live at home with their parents, or do they move away from their parents' house? Why?

2. Do you live with your parents now? Why or why not?

Watch the video once. Think about these questions:

1. How do the parents in the video feel?

2. Why do you think they feel this way?

Watch the video again. This time, watch for gestures. Put a check mark every time you see one of these gestures. You might want to watch several times to catch all of the gestures.

body movement

Gesture	Number of Times
Shaking hands	x
Kissing	1
Hugging	4
Holding hands	2
Putting an arm around each other	1

Think about a time you had to leave your family and friends. Talk about it with a few classmates.

1. Why did you have to leave? Talk about the reasons.

2. How did you feel?

3. How did your family and friends feel?

In the video, you see a student pretending to call his parents. Do you ever call your family or friends far away? It's wonderful to talk to them, but phone calls can be very expensive! Work with a partner. Pretend to call someone who is far away now. Tell this person about your life and your studies (in English, please). Then switch roles.

Being a new student at a new school can be difficult. Work in a small group. Think about advice you can give a new student. Complete the sentences below. Then share the sentences with your class.

Advice to New Students
You must . . . _____ *try to make new friends.* _____
You should . . . _____
You could . . . _____
You might . . . _____
You may . . . _____

PUTTING IT ALL TOGETHER

Write About It.

In a journal entry or letter to your teacher, write about something that surprised you or interested you in this chapter:

_____

_____

_____

_____

_____

_____

_____

_____

◆Outside Activity

1. Go to a place outside your classroom where there are many people speaking English—for example, the student activity center, a cafeteria, or a mall. Or, if you are not in an English-speaking country, watch television or films in English.

2. Watch and listen to people as they greet each other. Try to see at least five different greetings.

3. Take notes on what you hear and what you see.

What You Hear	What You See
1. Hi! How are you?	Smile and hug.
2.	
3.	
4.	
5.	

With a small group, share what you saw and heard. Which greetings seem formal? Why? Which greetings seem informal? Why?

◆More Practice

Choose one or more of these activities:

1. As you leave class today, say "Good-bye" to your teacher and call him or her by the correct name.

2. Tell a classmate the names of all of your classes and teachers.

3. Introduce yourself to a native speaker.

4. Exchange greetings with someone on campus.

Test-Taking Tip

During a speaking test, you need to speak! Try to give interesting answers, not just "yes" or "no." Remember that your instuctor is asking you questions because she or he wants to listen to you. Try to give full answers and show your instructor that you want to speak.

CHECK YOUR PROGRESS

On a scale of 1 to 5, where 1 means "not at all," 2 means "not very well," 3 means "moderately well," 4 means "well," and 5 means "very well," rate how well you have mastered the goals set at the beginning of the chapter:

1 2 3 4 5   introduce yourself and others in both formal and informal ways.

1 2 3 4 5   practice speaking English with classmates.

1 2 3 4 5   use appropriate body language when meeting and greeting people.

1 2 3 4 5   make connections between new things and familiar words and ideas.

1 2 3 4 5   greet people in both formal and informal ways.

1 2 3 4 5   understand and pronounce reductions correctly.

1 2 3 4 5   address your teachers appropriately.

If you've given yourself a 3 or lower on any of these goals:

- visit the *Tapestry* web site for additional practice.
- ask your instructor for extra help.
- review the sections of the chapter that you found difficult.
- work with a partner or study group to further your progress.

L ook at these photos. Discuss these questions with your classmates:

• What is happening in each of these photos?
• Have you ever been in one of these situations? When? What happened?

FINDING YOUR WAY

This chapter will help you find your way (without getting lost!). You will learn how to get around where you live while you are driving or walking. Also, you will learn more about finding your way on a college campus. Finally, you will learn what to do if you feel lost in the classroom.

Setting Goals

In this chapter you will learn to:

- understand and give directions.
- read a campus map.
- use prepositions of direction.
- use movement to remember what you hear.
- get to know campus resources.
- ask for clarification when you don't understand someone.
- pronounce syllables and stress correctly.
- pronounce new words.

◆**Getting Started**

Work with a partner. Read the statements about cars in the thread on the following page. Fill in the blanks with your guesses. Then look at the bottom of the page for the answers.

1. How close were your guesses?

2. Which statistic is the most surprising? Why?

3. Which statistic is the most interesting? Why?

PART 1: Finding Your Way in the World

Culture Note

Cars are an important part of North American culture. For many people, having a car means having personal freedom. With a car, you can go anywhere you want, anytime you want. Getting a first car is a big event for many teenagers.

◆**Getting Ready to Read**

Discuss these questions with a partner:

1. What are the benefits, or good points, of public transportation?

2. What different types of public transportation are you familiar with?

◆**Read**

*rural
an eara
far from the city*

1 Cars are too expensive for many people around the world to own. Not only that, many cities are already full of traffic, and many **rural** areas have rough roads (and few **mechanics**!).

In 1895 there were about 300 cars in the United States.

In 1995 there were about _____ cars in the United States.

The average price of a new car in 1917 was $720.

The average price of a new car in 1997 was $ _____.

In 1990 the number of Americans who walked to work was 4,500,000.

In 1990 the number of Americans who drove to work was _____.

—DANIEL P. GEORGE

2   So how do people travel those distances that are too far to walk? They use public transportation. If you ride the subway or bus where you live, you can **appreciate** some of the benefits of public transportation. With many people sharing one bus or train, there is less **traffic** and, more importantly, less **pollution.**

3   Which of the types of **mass transit** described below are you familiar with?

4   If a regular bus can hold **dozens** of people, imagine what a bus twice the size can hold! In Great Britain, there are many buses that are known as double-deckers.

5   Buses in Haiti are often very crowded. It's not uncommon for passengers to actually sit on the rooftops. Buses are affectionately called "tap-taps," because the riders on the roof tap when they want to be **dropped off.**

In 1990 the number of Americans who drove to work was 99,600,000.
The average price of a new car in 1997 was $22,450.
In 1995 there were about 136,000,000 cars in the United States.

test

take advantage of = use influence.

(MPH) = miles per hour

6   Many large cities around the world **take advantage of** the space beneath the streets and run underground trains. People in Paris, Mexico City, and Tokyo may use the subway system to get to school, to work, or to visit friends in other neighborhoods.

7   Both the Japanese and French have developed high-speed trains **to link** various cities. While electric trains in North America average 80 mph (130 kph), the French TGV (for *train a grand vitesse*, French for high-speed train) is the world's fastest, averaging over 170 mph (270 kph)!

◆ Vocabulary Building

Look in the reading for the vocabulary on the left. Then, match the meaning of each word or phrase with the definition on the right.

_b_ 1. rural	a. the flow of cars, buses, etc.
_e_ 2. mechanic	b. related to the countryside, not the city
_h_ 3. to appreciate	c. groups of 12, often used to express large amounts
_a_ 4. traffic	d. to stop and let someone out of a vehicle
_j_ 5. pollution	e. someone who repairs or fixes cars
_i_ 6. mass transit	f. to use an opportunity
_c_ 7. dozens	g. to join two things together
_d_ 8. to drop off	h. to understand the value of something
_f_ 9. to take advantage of	i. transportation for a large number of people
_g_ 10. to link	j. impurities, such as chemicals, that make water, air, and soil dirty

After You Read

Answer these questions:

1. What are two benefits of public transportation?

2. Why are buses in Haiti called "tap-taps"?

3. What are some of the cities that have a subway system?

4. Where can you find the world's fastest train?

5. What types of mass transit, or public transportation, are common in your native country?

6. Do you prefer to drive a car, take a bus, ride a subway, or take a train? Why?

TUNING IN: "The Sparrow"

You will learn about a new type of transportation called a Sparrow. Before you watch, think about cars and motorcycles. Put an X for each statement that is true for cars and motorcycles. Leave the third column blank. Discuss your answers with classmates.

© CNN

it's a bike

	CARS	MOTORCYCLES	SPARROW
Easy to park	____	✓	✓
Cheap to buy	____	✓	____
Cheap to drive	____	✓	____
Uses gas	✓	✓	____
Uses electricity	✓	____	✓
Warm and dry in all weather	✓	____	has t
Easy to use in traffic	____	✓	____
Safe to drive	✓	____	____
Can carry a passenger	✓	✓	____

As you watch, put an X for each statement that is true about the Sparrow. You may want to watch twice. Compare your answers with classmates.

Electric cars are not new to the United States. The first American Company to manufacture electric cars was Woods Motor Vehicle Co. in 1896. By 1904, about one-third of all cars in the United States were electric. But eventually electric cars lost out to gas powered cars. By the 1930's, there were no companies manufacturing electric cars.

What type of transportation do you think is best, a car, a motor-cycle, or a Sparrow? Why? Tell a partner what you think.

Getting Ready to Listen

You will hear directions from San Francisco, California, to West Valley Community College in Saratoga, California. Look at the map of the Bay Area. Before you listen, predict the best way to drive. Explain to a partner how to drive from San Francisco to WVCC.

Listen

Listening 1: Following Directions

As you listen to the directions, draw a line on the map. Now listen again. Fill in the blanks with one of the words below:

highway	go	south	two	continue
exit	take	onto	turn	
miles	make	for	right	

From San Francisco, _____take_____ highway 101 _____south_____. _____Continue_____ south for approximately 20 _____miles_____. Then, take _____Highway_____ 85 south. _____Go_____ south on 85 _____for_____ about 7 miles. Take the

Saratoga Ave. _____*exit*_____ west. Continue
on Saratoga Ave. for _____*two*_____ blocks.
_____*turn*_____ left at the first traffic signal
_____*onto*_____ Fruitvale Ave. _____*Make*_____
another left on Allendale Ave. past the church. Take the second
_____*right*_____ into the campus parking lot.

◀After You Listen

Discuss these questions with your classmates:

1. How do you get to school? By car? By bus? By foot?

2. Do you have a car? Why or why not?

3. Is the public transportation system in your area good? Why or why not?

LANGUAGE YOU CAN USE: GIVING DIRECTIONS

Here are some expressions you can use to give directions:

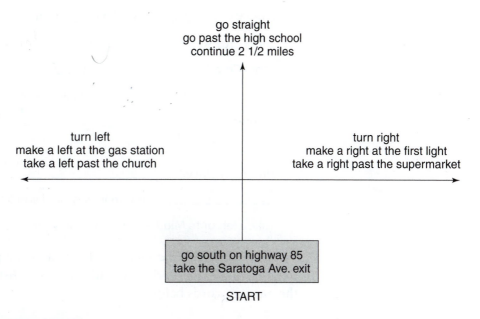

go straight
go past the high school
continue 2 1/2 miles

turn left
make a left at the gas station
take a left past the church

turn right
make a right at the first light
take a right past the supermarket

go south on highway 85
take the Saratoga Ave. exit

START

USING NEW LANGUAGE

Use the map on the next page of a small city in Northern California. Practice giving directions with a partner.

test

CIVIC CENTER/DOWNTOWN
VALPARAISO AVE.

blue you can faster travel

Partner A Give the directions on p. 275 to your partner. Remember to read then look up at your partner and give directions.

Partner B Look at the map and listen as your partner gives directions from the train depot to Nealon Park. Then listen again and fill in the missing words below:

From the train depot you want to ____take____

Santa Cruz Ave. toward El Camino Real. ____follow____

Santa Cruz Ave. for about ____a half____ ____mile____

_____. You'll pass many stores and a bank

on the ____left____. ____take a____

____left____ _____ on

University Drive. ____go____ ____four____ ____blocks____

_____ on University until you get to Middle Ave.

Take a left onto Middle. The park is on your ____left____.

Partner A Look at the map and listen as your partner gives directions from Nealon Park to the library. Then listen again and fill in the missing words below:

From Nealon Park, _____ Middle Ave.

toward El Camino Real. _____ _____

onto El Camino and go _____ blocks. Take

a _____ at Ravenswood. You'll know it

because you'll see a big bookstore on the corner of Ravenswood and El Camino. Take the _____ _____

past the railroad tracks. That's Alma. The library is on Alma, on

your _____ .

Partner B Give the directions on p. 276 to your partner. Remember to read then look up at your partner and give directions.

Write About It.

Use the map of Menlo Park on page 34. Give directions from Burgess Park to the post office. Write them here:

Take Laurel N, pas. D. st. and Ravens. w'ood Ave. until you get to. oak grove, make a left, you go E. pass el camino Rd., the post office is the first building on the left, past maloney

PART 2: Finding Your Way on Campus

A CAMPUS MAP

You will read a campus map. The campus map is a grid. It has numbers on the left side and letters on the bottom. Do you know how to read a grid? Show a classmate.

1. Point to A4.   2. Point to G2.   3. Point to C7-8.

Grid →

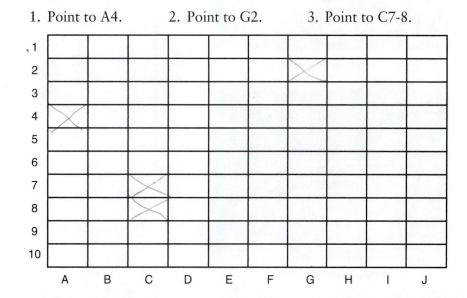

Campus Center Walk

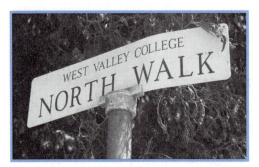

North Walk

Language Arts

Bridge at North Walk

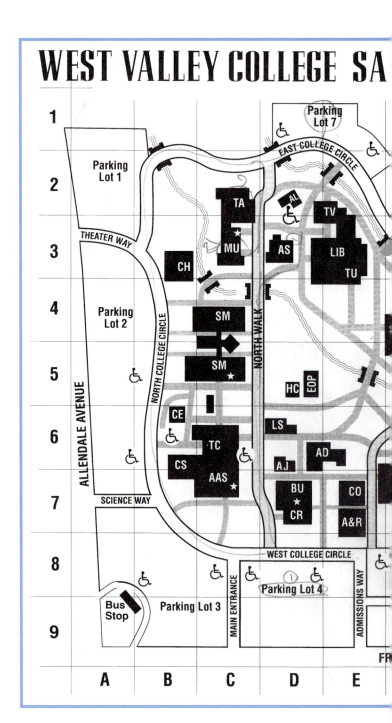

TOGA, CALIFORNIA

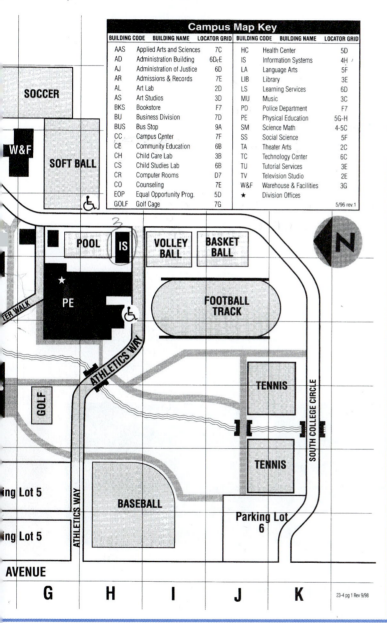

Campus Map Key

BUILDING CODE	BUILDING NAME	LOCATOR GRID	BUILDING CODE	BUILDING NAME	LOCATOR GRID
AAS	Applied Arts and Sciences	7C	HC	Health Center	5D
AD	Administration Building	6D-E	IS	Information Systems	4H
AJ	Administration of Justice	6D	LA	Language Arts	5F
AR	Admissions & Records	7E	LIB	Library	3E
AL	Art Lab	2D	LS	Learning Services	6D
AS	Art Studios	3D	MU	Music	3C
BKS	Bookstore	F7	PD	Police Department	F7
BU	Business Division	7D	PE	Physical Education	5G-H
BUS	Bus Stop	9A	SM	Science Math	4-5C
CC	Campus Center	7F	SS	Social Science	5F
CE	Community Education	6B	TA	Theater Arts	2C
CH	Child Care Lab	3B	TC	Technology Center	6C
CS	Child Studies Lab	6B	TU	Tutorial Services	3E
CR	Computer Rooms	D7	TV	Television Studio	2E
CO	Counseling	7E	W&F	Warehouse & Facilities	3G
EOP	Equal Opportunity Prog.	5D	★	Division Offices	
GOLF	Golf Cage	7G			5/96 rev.1

SOCCER

W&F

SOFT BALL

POOL IS VOLLEY BALL BASKET BALL

N

★ PE

FOOTBALL TRACK

ATHLETICS WAY

GOLF

TENNIS

SOUTH COLLEGE CIRCLE

TENNIS

ing Lot 5

ATHLETICS WAY

BASEBALL

Parking Lot 6

ing Lot 5

AVENUE

G   H   I   J   K

23-4 pg 1 Rev 9/98

Administration Building

Campus Center

Language Arts

Applied Arts and Sciences

disc ✗

Work with a partner. Look at the campus map and the map key and answer the questions:

1. You will find the ___PE___ building in 5G-H.
2. The library is in ___3E___.
3. Parking lot 1 is in ___2A___.
4. The building code for the Bookstore is ___BKS___.
5. How many parking lots are there? There are ___7___.

Getting Ready to Listen

You will hear a new student ask for directions on campus. Write some phrases you can use to ask directions.

excuse me, could you tell me where the
library is.
How can I find the library?
Where can I find the library

Now write some phrases you can use to give directions.

_____

_____

_____

_____

Listen

Listening 2: Asking for Directions

Listen to the conversation. Fill in the blanks.

New Student:	Excuse me? Can you tell me how to get to the Language Arts building?

cross (v.)
across (adj)
crossroad (N)
what's your
cross street.

Student: Sure. _falow_ Campus Center Walk _past_ the Campus Center. Then, _bear (slight turn) the bear right_ onto the bridge.

New student: I'm sorry. Bear right?

Student: _walk_ a little to the _right_ but don't turn _right_ all the way. _tak Left_ a _the b._ after the bridge. The Language Arts building is the _firs_ building on the _right_. It's _a___ _cross_ the Physical Education building.

New Student: OK. So I _Take the_ Campus Center Walk _past_ the Campus Center. I _'m bear right_ onto the bridge. I _turn_ _Left_ after the bridge, and it's the first building on the _right_.

Student: You got it!

New Student: Thanks a lot.

Student: No problem.

◄**After You Listen**

Discuss these questions with your classmates:

1. Did the new student understand everything the other student said?

2. What did the new student ask when he didn't understand?

3. What other expressions can you use when you don't understand someone?

If you travel or live in the United States or Canada you will discover that most people are happy to give directions. Asking for directions is a good way to practice English. Most people are very friendly and like to help.

Test

LANGUAGE YOU CAN USE: PREPOSITIONS OF DIRECTION

When you give directions, you often use prepositions of direction.

The words below are prepositions of direction. You can use them to give directions:

PREPOSITION OF DIRECTION	EXAMPLES
near	There is a post office near the apartments.
across from	We have a park across from our apartment building.
next to	The fruit stand is next to the radio station.
in front of	The bus is in front of the school.
behind	There is a water tower behind the post office.
close to	The burger place is close to the school.
around the corner from	Around the corner from the radio station is the church.

S
icon
icons
p

I conict mek

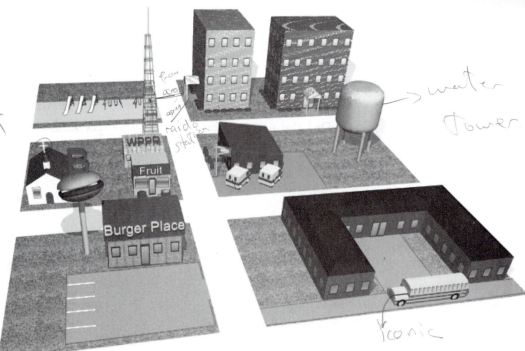

◆ Where Is the Destination?

You will hear directions to other buildings on campus. Use the campus map on pages 36 and 37. Listen and follow the directions on the map. Where is the destination? Circle it.

1.

    a. Library (LIB)

    b. Television Studio (TV)

    c. Music (MU)

2.

    a. Science Math (SM)

    b. Theater Arts (TA)

    c. Art Studios (AS)

3.

    a. Language Arts (LA)

    b. Physical Education (PE)

    c. Information Services (IS)

> **Women tend to navigate by landmarks and visual memories. Men tend to navigate by direction and distance, and tend to be more map-oriented.**

USING NEW LANGUAGE

Work with a partner. Use the campus map on pages 36 and 37. Student A, ask the questions below. Student B, answer by completing the directions.

Question: (in front of the Campus Center)
                Excuse me. Can you tell me how to get to the library?
Directions: Sure, it's easy. Just go . . .

Question: (in front of the library)
              Pardon me. Where is the Administration building?
Directions: Oh. You're close now. Walk . . .

Now Student B, ask the questions below. Student A, answer by completing the directions.

Question: (in front of the Administration building)
              Hello. Do you know how to get to the pool from here?
Directions: Yeah. Continue . . .

Question: (in front of the pool)
              Sorry. Can you tell me where the Music building is?
Directions: The Music building? It's down near Parking Lot 1.
              Go . . .

Guess the Destination

Work in a group of four or five students.

1. Get a map of the campus where you study or the city where you live.

2. Take turns giving directions. Don't say the destination.

3. The first person to guess the destination gets one point.

4. The classmate with the most points wins the game.

LANGUAGE LEARNING STRATEGY

Use movement to learn new expressions that you hear. Learning a lot of new words and expressions can be difficult. Help your memory by using movement. Moving your body helps your brain remember more easily.

Apply the Strategy

Close your book and listen to your teacher. Follow her commands and have fun!

Now practice the expressions below with a partner. Take turns giving commands and following them:

turn left	go forward	stand next to the _____
turn right	stop	stand across from the _____
go straight	turn around	stand behind the _____

ACADEMIC POWER STRATEGY

Get to know campus resources. Getting to know the campus where you study is very useful. There are many organizations and departments on campus to help you. For example, if you are sick, you can go to the student health center. If you need help in a class, you can go to the tutoring center. Be a successful student. Learn where to go when you need assistance.

Apply the Strategy

West Valley College
Library Hours

Monday–Thursday
8am–9pm

Friday
8am–3:30pm

Saturday
Noon–4pm

Closed
Sunday and
College Holidays

Book Checkout Desk
741-2028

Audiovisual
Checkout Desk
741-2624

Periodicals
Checkout Desk
741-2644

Reference Desk
741-2029

www.westvalley.edu/wvc/pat/

You will go on a scavenger hunt with your classmates. A scavenger hunt is a game. The goal of the game is to find as many things on a list as possible. Whoever finds the most things on the list wins the game.

Find out (learn) more about your campus. Visit these places on campus in teams of two or three. Pick up the items on the list. The first team to finish wins!

1. A campus map (hint: try the information desk)

2. A handout from the library

3. A health brochure from the student health center

4. An information flyer from the campus police department

5. A handout from the tutoring center(s)

6. A list of student organizations/clubs on campus

Share what you find with your classmates.

PART 3: Finding Your Way in the Classroom

LANGUAGE YOU CAN USE: ASKING FOR CLARIFICATION

che

> The techniques of opening conversation are universal. I knew long ago and rediscovered that the best way to attract attention, help, and conversation is to be lost. A man will cheerfully devote several hours of his time giving wrong directions to a total stranger who claims to be lost.
>
> **—JOHN STEINBECK**

Sometimes you don't understand or don't hear someone clearly. Native speakers sometimes have trouble understanding each other, too! When you don't understand or hear someone clearly, you must ask for clarification. "To clarify" means to check your understanding. It also means to ask the speaker to speak more clearly. Asking for clarification will help you when you feel lost in the classroom. It will also help outside the classroom.

Here are some expressions to use when asking for clarification:

ASKING FOR CLARIFICATION	EXAMPLE
say that again	
(Would/could/can) you say that again?	Could you say that again?
(Would/could/can) you repeat that?	Would you please repeat that?
Did you say ___goulash___ ?	Did you say "bear right"?
What does ___bear right___ mean?	What does "bear right" mean?
I'm sorry, ___bear right___ ?	I'm sorry, "bear right"?

what does Pageant mean?

USING NEW LANGUAGE

I'm sorry = pardon me

1) I didn't hear what you said

2) I didn't understand?

Listen to your teacher give directions from your school to the local library or other location. Take notes. Raise your hand and ask for clarification when you do not understand something.

_____

_____

_____

_____

Did you ask for clarification? Great!

Now practice with a partner. Your partner will give you directions from his or her home or job to school. Listen and take notes. Remember to ask for clarification when you do not understand something.

(handwritten top margin: what Time is   reverse ⟳   forbiten)

_____

_____

_____

_____

Did you use some of the new expressions from Language You Can Use? Put a check mark next to the expressions you used.

◆ **Interview**

(handwritten: make the question)

(handwritten: P. A)

Work with a partner to learn more about campus resources. Student A, practice forming questions about the campus bookstore using the chart below. Student B, look at the chart on the next page. Now Student A, interview Student B about the campus bookstore. Fill in the chart with the answers. Remember to ask for clarification.

Questions	Campus Bookstore	Student Health Center
what/hours?	_could you please tell me what are the hours of the cafeteria_ / _What are the hours of campus Bookstore?_	Monday–Thursday 8 a.m.–6 p.m. Friday 8 a.m.–5 p.m.
who/use?	_who use the campus Bookstore?_	Registered students
what/services?	_what kind of services it has?_	Checkups, visits with doctors and nurses to treat illness or injury, tests, medicine
what/cost?	_what does it cost?_	Checkups/visits: no fee Test/medicine: $25
what/phone number?	_what is the phone number?_	(650) 555-SICK (650) 555-7425

(handwritten right margin: cafeteria   7 am–7:45)

Now Student A, review the information above about the student health center. Answer Student B's questions using the information.

B P.

Student B, read the information below about the campus bookstore. Answer Student A's questions using the information in the chart.

Questions	Campus Bookstore	Student Health Center
what/hours?	Monday–Thursday 7:30 a.m.–7 p.m. Friday 7:30 a.m.–4 p.m.	*what are the hours of campus bookstore M–th. frida 8–5pm 8am–6pm*
who/use?	Anyone	*who use the campus Book store? registered students*
what/services?	Textbooks, class supplies, paperbacks, candy, computer software, clothes, magazines, gifts.	*what are the services of campus? Checkups, visits with doctors & nurse to treat illness or injury tests medicine*
what/cost?	Same as other bookstores for most items. 30% student discount on some items.	*What does it cost? checkup & visits no fee test/medicen $25*
what/phone number?	(650) 555-BOOK (650) 555-2665	*what's the phone number? (656)555 sick (650) 555 9425*

Now Student B, practice forming questions about the student health center using the chart above. Then interview Student A. Fill in the chart with the answers. Remember to ask for clarification.

The Sound of It: Syllable Stress

O T ut

English words can be divided into syllables. A syllable is a beat. If English was music, syllables would be the drums of English. For example, *syl la ble* has three syllables. Can you hear them? Be a drum. Use your foot to tap on the floor. Or use your pencil to tap the desk.

Listen as your teacher says these words. How many syllables do they have?

__1__ drive	walk	car
__2__ college	parking	commute
__3__ directions	professor	commuter
__4__ automobile	information	community
__5__ university	administration	opportunity

Listen for Syllables

Listen to the tape. Write the number of syllables next to each word. Remember to trust your ears, not your eyes!

_4_ television   _1_ class

_2_ campus   _3_ library

_3_ studio   _2_ study

Syllable Stress

Syllables are the drums of English. Some beats are loud, and some are not. We call the loud beats **stressed syllables.**

Listen to your teacher say this word *COL lege.*

- How many syllables are there?

- Which syllable is louder? *COL lege*

- Good. Now which syllable is longer? *COL lege*

- Which syllable is higher? *COL lege*

Stressed syllables are pronounced louder, longer, and higher than other syllables.

Go back to the words your teacher said on p. 46. Listen as your teacher says them again. Mark the stressed syllables.

Listen for Syllable Stress

Now listen to this radio commercial. Listen once and write the number of syllables you hear in each word in italics. Then listen again and mark the stressed syllable. The first one has been done for you.

Announcer:

Does this sound all too familiar? Are you one of the *millions* _2_ of Americans who spends too much time in your car *commuting* _3_ ? Well, the *Community* _4_ Transportation Service is here to help you. We have *information* _4_ about a variety of *transportation* _4_ alternatives. What about taking the *train* _1_ ? Riding the bus? Using your *bike* _1_ or your feet? We can give you *public* _2_ transportation information or help you find *people* _2_ to share the ride in your *automobile* _4_ .

Call now and let us help you escape from your car. It's free, and it could change your life! Call (650) COMMUTE. That's (650) 266-6883. Call now!

Pair Practice

Practice reading the commercial above and on the previous page. Partner A, read the commercial. Partner B, listen for the syllables and stress in the italicized words. Now switch and repeat.

LANGUAGE LEARNING STRATEGY

Learn how new words are pronounced. You are learning many new words in English. Sometimes, you *see* new words when you read, but you don't *hear* them. Listen to how new words are pronounced. You will hear them more easily when listening. You will also be able to use them correctly when you speak.

Learn these two things about the pronunciation of new words:

1. How many syllables there are—for example, there are three syllables in the word *syl la ble*.

2. Where the stress is—for example, the stress in *SYL la ble* is on the first syllable.

There are three ways to learn the number of syllables and stress in new words:

1. Listen for syllables and stress in new words.

2. Ask the teacher or your classmates.

3. Look in a dictionary.

> **syl•la•ble** /ˈsɪləbəl/ *n.* **1** a part of a word as determined by vowel sounds and rhythm: *"Cat" is a word of one syllable; "hotel" has two syllables.*

Apply the Strategy

Look through this chapter. Choose five words you have learned or want to learn this week. Write them on the following lines:

mark the number of syllables. Mark the syllable stress on each

_____

_____

_____

_____

_____

Now mark the number of syllables. Mark the syllable stress on each word. Practice saying the words correctly.

PUTTING IT ALL TOGETHER

 **Give Directions**

Work with a group of classmates. Take turns giving directions from where you study to your homes. Take notes.

 **Campus Interview**

Your teacher will assign you and a partner a resource on campus. You will interview the person working there. You will ask these questions. Practice asking the questions with a partner.

1. What are the hours here?

_____

2. Who can use the resources here?

_____

3. What services do you offer students?

_____

4. Is there a cost?

_____

5. What is the phone number here?

_____

Now go with your partner to interview the resource person. Remember to ask for clarification when you don't understand. Write down the answers.

Bring your notes to class. Give a report to your classmates.

◆ **Internet Campus Visit**

Many campuses have a web site on the Internet. You can visit a campus while you sit at your computer! Here are some interesting campus web sites:

West Valley Community College, Saratoga California
www.westvalley.edu

Foothill Community College, Los Altos Hills, California
www.foothill.fhda.edu

San Francisco State University
www.sfsu.edu

San Jose State University
www.sjsu.edu

Test-Taking Tip

Use your answer sheet correctly:

• Be sure you understand the correct way to mark your answers on the answer sheet. If you are not sure, ask your instructor.

• Choose the correct answer. Mark it in the right space on the answer sheet. Be sure to match the number on the answer sheet and the number of the question.

• If you skip a question on the test, be sure to skip the space for that question on the answer sheet.

CHECK YOUR PROGRESS

On a scale of 1 to 5, rate how well you have mastered the goals set at the beginning of the chapter:

1 2 3 4 5   understand and give directions.

1 2 3 4 5   read a campus map.

1 2 3 4 5   use prepositions of direction.

1 2 3 4 5   use movement to remember what you hear.

1 2 3 4 5   get to know campus resources.

1 2 3 4 5   ask for clarification when you don't understand someone.

1 2 3 4 5   pronounce syllables and stress correctly.

1 2 3 4 5   learn how to pronounce new words.

If you've given yourself a 3 or lower on any of these goals:

- visit the *Tapestry* web site for additional practice.
- ask your instructor for extra help.
- review the sections of the chapter that you found difficult.
- work with a partner or study group to further your progress.

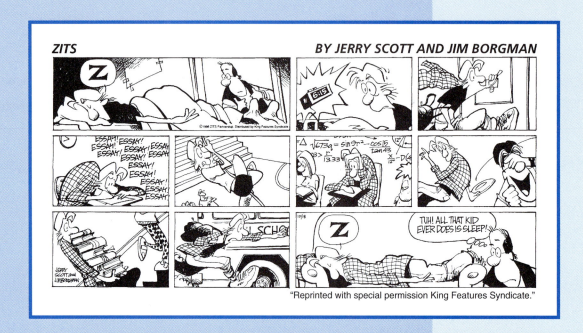

L ook at the cartoon. Discuss the questions below with a partner:

• Describe the student's day. What does he do every day?

• What does the student's father think about his life? What do you think about the student's life?

• Is your life similar to this student's life? How is your life similar or different?

A FULL LIFE

Most people have busy lives. We spend a lot of time working, studying, and taking care of family responsibilities. We also have some free time, time to relax. This time is very special because we don't have a lot! In this chapter, you will talk about how you spend your time. You will also talk about your free time and how you relax.

Setting Goals

In this chapter you will learn to:

◈ talk about your regular schedule.

◈ ask questions and participate in class.

◈ use adverbs of frequency.

◈ understand and pronounce sentence stress correctly.

◈ listen for the topic of conversations.

◈ start conversations with new people.

◈ join a club or group on campus.

◆ **Getting Started**

In the United States in 1995:
- **44% of all college students were over the age of 25.**
- **54% of all college students worked and studied at the same time.**
- **43% of all college students attended school part time.**

Read the statistics about college students. Find out more about your class. Take a poll.

- How many students in your class are over 25 years old?
- How many students in your class work and study at the same time?
- How many students in your class attend school part time?

YOUR CLASS

_____ % are over 25.

_____ % work and study.

_____ % attend school part time.

Compare the students in your class to the students in 1995. Are the students in your class similar or different?

PART 1: How Do You Spend Your Time?

◆ **Getting Ready to Read**

You will read about college students in the past, present, and future. Before you read, predict or guess what you will read. Check the statements you think are true:

_____ All college students are young.

_____ Many students study part time.

_____ Most students live in a dorm room.

_____ Taking a class through the Internet is common now.

_____ Many students work and study at the same time.

◆ **Vocabulary Building**

Read the sentences below. Then, as you listen, try to guess the meaning of the underlined vocabulary words and phrases.

1.

A: How was your day?

B: Oh, nothing special. It was a <u>typical</u> day.

Guess: _____

2.

A: Do you live off campus?

B: No. I live in a <u>dorm room</u> here on campus. It's very convenient.

Guess: _____

3.

A: Do you enjoy having a <u>roommate</u>?

B: Yeah. It's my first experience sharing a room, but it's really nice to have someone to talk to.

Guess: _____

4.

A: Do you need help choosing a major? Come to the <u>academic</u> counseling center. We can help you with school decisions.

B: Thanks. I think I'll come!

Guess: _____

5.

A: Teenagers in the United States are so <u>independent</u>.

B: It's true. They often move out of their parents' house when they go to college.

Guess: _____

6.

A: When I was a college student, all the students were young.

B: Yeah, I remember that, too. But these days, the student population is more <u>multigenerational</u>.

Guess: _____

7.

A: Did you go to the <u>multicultural</u> fair today?

B: Yeah. It was really interesting. I tried some Korean BBQ, had some Thai iced tea, and watched a Native American dance.

Guess: _____

8.

A: Did your mother have a professional <u>career</u>, or did she work at home?

B: Actually, she did both. When we were young, she stayed home. Later, she went back to school and became a lawyer.

Guess: _____

9.

A: Do you use the <u>Internet</u>?

B: Yes! I got a new computer for Christmas. Now I surf the net every night!

Guess: _____

10.

A: Have you ever taken a <u>distance learning</u> course?

B: Yes, just this past semester. I took a business class. Half the class met on this campus in a classroom while the professor and the other students were in a classroom across the country.

Guess: _____

Now match the vocabulary on the left with the definitions on the right.

1. typical

2. dorm room

3. roommate

4. academic

5. independent

6. multigenerational

7. multicultural

8. career

9. Internet

10. distance learning

a. a system of connected computers that allows computer users around the world to share information

b. related to studying and school, especially in a college or university

c. has the usual qualities of a thing, person, or group

d. a job or profession that you train for and do for a long time

e. free, not needing to ask other people for help, money, or permission to do something

f. a room in a large building at a school or college where students live

g. including people of many different ages

h. someone you share a room, apartment, or house with

i. a nontraditional way of studying, such as watching the instructor teach on a TV in another room in another place

j. including people from many different countries, races, or religions

Read

Students in the Past, Present, and Future

1   In the 1960s and 1970s, **typical** college students lived on the college campus. They attended classes full time. They were usually between eighteen and twenty-two years old. They went to college for four years. A typical day for students in the past was like this. They woke up in the **dorm room** they shared with a **roommate.** They ate breakfast in the school cafeteria. Then they went to classes. After classes, they studied in the library for a few hours. Maybe they went to a basketball game with friends at the gym. Perhaps they talked until late at night in their dorm rooms.

2   The life of a typical student was centered on the college campus. Social life was part of **academic** life. Students wanted to get a degree. But they also wanted to learn how to be **independent** adults.

3   The life of a college student has changed a lot since then. Although there are still many students who go to school full time and live on campus, many students don't. Today's students are often

older, working adults. These students usually study part time. They are **multigenerational** and **multicultural.** They work, and they go to school. They may also have children to take care of. They have a full and busy life outside of school. School is just one part of their lives, not the center of their lives. They go to school to learn new skills for their jobs, to get better jobs, or to change **careers.** Some students go to school simply because they want to keep learning.

4   What about the future? Well, there will be no such thing as a typical student. Most people will take classes at some time in their lives. People will study when they need to. They will study just to learn when they get older.

5   And where will they study? In the future, most students will not go to school. School will come to the students. Colleges will offer more classes in the workplace. People will be able to study and work without getting in the car. **Internet** classes will be more common. People will be able to sit at a computer anywhere in the world and study. **Distance learning** will be more common, too. Using special televisions, students will take classes with teachers all over the world. Studying at work, on the Internet, and through distance learning is possible now. But in the future, it will probably be more common.

 **After You Read**

Work with a partner. Discuss these questions:

1. What was a typical student like in the past?

2. What is a typical student like now?

3. How will people study in the future?

Work in a small group. Share your opinions.

1. Is it better to study full time or part time? Why?

2. Is it better to live on campus or off campus? Why?

3. Is it better to work while you study or not work while you study? Why?

TUNING IN: "Going Back to School"

© CNN

In the video, you will learn that 5 million adults over the age of 25 are going back to school. Why do you think so many adults go back to school? Talk to a partner about your ideas.

As you watch, check off the reasons you hear.

Older adults are going back to school . . .

_____ to have something to do

_____ to succeed at work

_____ to get a better job

_____ to keep learning

_____ because colleges and universities are trying to get older students to come

_____ to learn the newest information for their jobs

Watch again. Think about this question and check your answer: How do teachers feel about having older students in their classes?

_____ They like having older students.

_____ They don't like having older students.

Why do you think the teachers feel that way?

Getting Ready to Listen   You will hear two students meet on campus. They will talk about their schedules. Before you listen, talk to a partner about his or her regular schedule:

1. How many classes are you taking now?

2. Do you work? If so, how many hours per week?

3. Do you feel busy? Why or why not?

Listen

Listening 1: Talking About Schedules

Circle the correct answers while you listen.

1. Khaled is
   a. busy.
   b. not busy.

2. Khaled works
   a. every weekday.
   b. on Tuesday and Thursday.

3. Marina is on campus
   a. Tuesday and Thursday mornings.
   b. Tuesday and Thursday afternoons.

4. Khaled and Marina will meet
   a. on Friday at noon.
   b. on Friday in the afternoon.

After You Listen

Discuss these questions with a classmate from another culture, if possible:

1. In your native culture, can a man and a woman be friends?

2. When you make plans for coffee with someone of the opposite sex, is it a romantic date or a friendly appointment?

3. In the dialogue, did Khaled and Marina make a friendly appointment or a romantic date? Why do you think this?

> There can't be a crisis next week. My schedule is already full.
>
> —HENRY KISSINGER

LANGUAGE YOU CAN USE:
TALKING ABOUT YOUR REGULAR SCHEDULE

When we talk about our regular schedule, we often use these time expressions:

EXPRESSIONS	EXAMPLE
On Tuesdays and Thursdays	*On Tuesdays and Thursdays,* I go to the gym.
Every Monday, Wednesday, and Friday	*Every Monday, Wednesday, and Friday,* I have classes.

EXPRESSIONS	EXAMPLE
In the morning (afternoon, evening)	*In the morning,* I do housework. I work at the store *in the afternoon.*
During the week	I go to school *during the week.*
On the weekends	*On the weekends,* I hang out with friends.
On Saturdays	I go to the movies *on Saturdays.*

USING NEW LANGUAGE

Work with a partner. Use the new expressions to talk about student schedules.

Student A: Look at p. 273. Use the new expressions to make sentences about Jorge's regular schedule.

Student B: Listen to Student A tell you about Jorge's regular schedule. Fill in the schedule below.

	SUN	MON	TUES	WED	THUR	FRI	SAT
M O R N I N G							
A F T E R N O O N							
E V E N I N G							

Now student B look at p. 274. Then use the new expressions to make sentences about Makito's regular schedule.

Student A: Listen to Student A tell you about Makito's regular schedule. Fill in the schedule on the next page.

	SUN	MON	TUES	WED	THUR	FRI	SAT
M O R N I N G							
A F T E R N O O N							
E V E N I N G							

◆ **Pair Practice**   1. Now fill in the schedule below with your regular activities.

	SUN	MON	TUES	WED	THUR	FRI	SAT
M O R N I N G							
A F T E R N O O N							
E V E N I N G							

2. Work with a partner. Tell each other about your schedules.

3. Take notes.

4. Then give a short presentation to a small group about your partner's regular schedule.

5. Your classmates should write down the time expressions you use.

Write About It.

Write a short paragraph (at least ten sentences) about your regular schedule. Be sure to use some of the time expressions from Language You Can Use.

_____

_____

_____

_____

_____

_____

_____

_____

_____

_____

LANGUAGE LEARNING STRATEGY

To learn English, you must ask questions and participate in the classroom. Learn how to ask questions in your English class, and you will learn more quickly and easily.

Here are some helpful questions:

How do you spell _____?

What does _____ mean?

What's the meaning of _____?

Can you repeat that?

Can you please speak more slowly?

Can you please speak more loudly?

How do you pronounce _____?

(continued on next page)

Apply the Strategy

Play a game. Stand in front of your chair. Listen as your teacher tells you about his or her regular schedule. Raise your hand and ask one of the questions from above when you don't understand or when you want more information. When you have asked a question, you can sit down. Play until all students have an opportunity to ask a question.

This week, ask at least one question in each class. Put a check mark next to the questions you use. Try to use a new question each time.

Culture Note

Some people really like to get up early in the morning. They enjoy being awake before the rest of the world. They also get a lot of work done early in the day. We call these kinds of people *morning people*.

Other people like to sleep late. They enjoy being awake at night when the rest of the world is sleeping. They get a lot of work done late at night. These people are called *night owls*.

 Getting Ready to Listen

Ask a classmate these questions:

1. Are you a morning person or a night owl?

2. When do you do your best studying or work, in the morning or at night?

 Listen

Listening 2: Morning Person or Night Owl?

Listen to a conversation between two students, Alex and Manuel. Then fill in the blanks.

Alex: Manuel, you're not going home now, are you?

Manuel: Sorry! I have to get up early in the morning.

Alex: But it's only eleven o'clock!

Manuel: I'm _____ asleep by eleven!

Alex: Not me. I _____ stay up late.
           I _____ work late at night.

Manuel: You must be a real night owl. I guess I'm a morning person.

Alex: A morning person?

Manuel: Yeah. I _____ get up early in the morning. I _____ study for a few hours in the morning before I go to work.

Alex: Oh. I _____ study in the morning.
           My brain doesn't work that early!

Manuel: And I _____ study at night!

**After You Listen**

Have you ever had a job or responsibility where you had to work very early or very late? Did you like that schedule? Why or why not?

LANGUAGE YOU CAN USE: ADVERBS OF FREQUENCY

When you talk about your regular activities and things you do in your free time, you will often use adverbs of frequency. Look at the list of common adverbs of frequency. Then work with a partner to fill in the chart.

COMMON ADVERBS OF FREQUENCY

sometimes	_always_	most frequent
often	_____	↑
never	_____	
always	_____	
usually	_____	↓
rarely	_____	least frequent

Here are some examples:

They *always* come on time.   I *usually* stay up late.
No, I *rarely* jog.   We *never* study on Saturday.
Do you *often* jog?   He is* *sometimes* late to class.

USING NEW LANGUAGE

Finish these sentences with information about yourself. Share your sentences with several other classmates.

I always _____

I usually _____

I often _____

*The adverb always comes *before* the main verb except with the verb *to be*, where it comes *after*.

I sometimes _____

I rarely _____

I never _____

PART 2: How Do You Relax?

◆ **Interest Quiz**   What do you like to do when you have free time? Check off what you do often, sometimes, and never.

OFTEN	SOMETIMES	NEVER	STAYING AT HOME
_____	_____	_____	watch videos
_____	_____	_____	read books, magazines, or newspapers
_____	_____	_____	listen to music
_____	_____	_____	have dinner parties
_____	_____	_____	watch TV
_____	_____	_____	play board games

OFTEN	SOMETIMES	NEVER	SPORTS
_____	_____	_____	play soccer
_____	_____	_____	play basketball
_____	_____	_____	play football
_____	_____	_____	play Frisbee
_____	_____	_____	play golf
_____	_____	_____	swim
_____	_____	_____	run around a track
_____	_____	_____	go to the gym
_____	_____	_____	jog in the park
_____	_____	_____	play tennis

OFTEN	SOMETIMES	NEVER	GOING OUT
_____	_____	_____	go to the movies
_____	_____	_____	go dancing
_____	_____	_____	go to dinner
_____	_____	_____	go to a club

OFTEN	SOMETIMES	NEVER	PRACTICING HOBBIES
_____	_____	_____	collect stamps
_____	_____	_____	work in the garden
_____	_____	_____	take pictures
_____	_____	_____	sing in a group

All work and no play makes Jack a dull boy.

—ANONYMOUS

Discussion

Work with three other students. Compare your interest quiz with them. Make sentences about each other and yourself. For example:

I never play golf, but he often plays golf.

We all usually listen to music at night.

They often go to the movies on the weekend.

The Sound of It: Sentence Stress

Listen to these sentences. Which words are louder, higher, longer, and clearer?

we LOVE to GO to the MOVIES.

we OFTEN GO on the WEEKEND.

our FAVORITE MOVIE is STAR WARS.

The words that are louder, higher, longer, and clearer are STRESSED. The other words are unstressed.

Look at the sentences again. What words are stressed? What words are unstressed? Write them in the columns below.

Stressed Words	Unstressed Words
love	we

Content Words and Function Words

Stressed words are called **content words.** Content words carry the meaning in sentences. Content words are:

> nouns (*movies, Star Wars*)
>
> verbs (*watches, go*)
>
> adjectives (*great, romantic*)
>
> adverbs (*very, sometimes*)
>
> numbers (*ten, five*)

questions words (*where, who*)

Unstressed words are called **function words.** Function words are:

> forms of *to be* (*is, being*)
>
> prepositions (*into, for*)
>
> articles (*a, the*)
>
> pronouns (*he, his, us*)
>
> common conjunctions (*and, so*)

Look at these sentences:

> LOVE GO MOVIES.
>
> OFTEN GO WEEKEND.
>
> FAVORITE MOVIE STAR WARS.

These aren't written in correct English, but you can understand the meaning because content words are the *meaning* words. That is why content words get stressed. They are important. When you speak, stress content words. You will be easy to understand. When you listen, listen for content words. You will understand more easily.

Sentence Stress Practice

Read the dialogue aloud. Underline the *content* words.

Mio: Do you like to play sports?
Lissy: Yes. I often play sports on the weekend.
Mio: What kind of sports do you play?
Lissy: I play soccer with friends on Saturdays. On Sundays I sometimes go on hikes in the mountains.

Now listen to check your answers. Can you hear the stressed words?

Dialogue Practice

With a partner, write a dialogue about your interests and free time. Then practice your dialogue. Pronounce the stressed words louder, longer, higher, and more clearly. Present the dialogue to your classmates.

A: _____

B: _____

A: _____

B: _____

A: _____

B: _____

A: _____

B: _____

Many businesses have automated phone services. When you call, you hear a recorded message that gives you information and instructions. This can be a great way to practice listening to English and following instructions. No one knows if you make a mistake. (You can't make a mistake listening!)

 **Getting Ready to Listen**

Have you ever called an automated phone service? Tell a partner about your experience. Was it difficult to understand? Was it helpful?

 Listen

Listening 3: An Automated Phone Service

You will listen to Moviefone. Moviefone is a free telephone service in the United States. You can call to find out about movies playing in your area. On the following page, circle the number you will press.

Call 777-FILM or Visit MovieLink.com

1. Find movie showtimes, local theater information and even buy movie tickets over the phone and on the web.

2. Search for a film by title, theater or type of movie. On MovieLink.com, even search by star name or time of day.

3. Enter your 5-digit zip code to find the theaters nearest you.

4. Hear previews of movies on MovieFone or watch movie trailers, view posters and read about upcoming movies on MovieLink.com.

5. Enter a three digit Express Code for express access to your favorite theater. Don't know the code? Visit MovieLink.com for a complete list of codes.

TIP: Press ✱ once on MovieFone to repeat or change your previous selection. To start over, press ✱ three times.

777-FILM and MovieLink.com: For Movies, Showtimes, Even Tickets

©1998 MovieFone Inc. All rights reserved. Nasdaq: MOFN   SF 8/98

1. To choose from a list of current movies, press

2. To choose *Titanic*, press

3. To hear a list of theaters showing *Titanic*, press

4. To choose Century 12 in Redwood City, press

5. To find out show times, press

After You Listen

Talk to a few classmates. Discuss automatic telephone services. What are some advantages, or good points? What are some disadvantages, or negative points? Make a short list.

Advantages	Disadvantages
You can't make a mistake.	You can't talk to a real person.

PART 3: How Do You Talk to New People?

Small talk with strangers is an interesting part of life in the United States. People often have short conversations with people they don't know—for example, when sitting on the bus, waiting in line, or walking down the street. In fact, if you and the other person are the only people around, not talking to someone can be impolite.

◆Getting Ready to Listen

You will hear small talk between people who don't know each other very well. What topics do you think they will discuss? Put a check mark next to each topic you think they might talk about.

_____ weather

_____ politics

_____ work

_____ appearance

_____ money

_____ religion

_____ school

_____ popular culture

LANGUAGE LEARNING STRATEGY

Listen for the topic or subject of a conversation. You do not need to understand every word you hear to understand the topic. Start by listening for content words. You can practice listening for the topic wherever people are speaking English.

Apply the Strategy

You will hear four conversations. Listen for the topic of each conversation. Write the topic you hear.

Listen

Listening 4: Listen for the Topic

Conversation One (at a bus stop)

_____

Conversation Two (at a party)

_____

Conversation Three (in a café)

_____

Conversation Four (in line at a movie theater)

_____

Listen again to the conversations. This time, listen for the expression the first speaker uses to start the conversation.

Conversation One

_____

Conversation Two

_____

Conversation Three

_____

Conversation Four

_____

After You Listen

Return to the list of possible topics on page 71. Answer these questions:

1. What topics were discussed?

2. What topics were not discussed? Why do you think people who don't know each other might not discuss these topics?

3. In your first language, what topics are used for talking to new people?

4. Are the topics you just heard similar or different to the topics in your first language? How are they similar or different?

LANGUAGE YOU CAN USE: STARTING CONVERSATIONS WITH NEW PEOPLE

There are many ways to begin conversations with new people. Here are three good ways. First, you can talk about a shared situation. Second, you can talk about the weather. Third, you can ask about something the person is holding or wearing. Here are some examples of conversation starters:

A SHARED SITUATION

(at a party)	Isn't this a great song?
(at a friend's house)	How do you know Martin?
(waiting for an elevator)	This elevator is always so slow.
(the first day of class)	Are you a new student, too?

THE WEATHER

(sitting in a park)	Nice day, isn't it?
(riding on a bus)	What a beautiful day!
(walking through campus)	Brrr! It's really cold today.

WHAT SOMEONE IS HOLDING OR WEARING

(sitting in a café)	Is that a good book?
(waiting in an office)	That's a beautiful scarf.

USING NEW LANGUAGE

With a partner, create a role play for each of the following situations:

Situation One: You are in a gym. You see another student from your class.

Situation Two: You are the only passenger on a bus. Another person gets on and sits near you.

Situation Three: You are waiting for an elevator. Someone else comes to wait.

Situation Four: You are in a friend's dorm room. A new person enters the room.

In the United States, there are some topics you should not discuss with people you don't know well. These topics are politics, religion, money, and sex. You should also not ask personal questions about some-one's age or marital status. Finally, you should not talk about the person's weight or height. These topics are considered too serious or personal to discuss with a new person.

ACADEMIC POWER STRATEGY

Join a club or group on campus. This is a great way to be a more successful student. Join a club that does something you really like to do. This will help you to focus on the activity, not on speaking English. Joining a club on campus will help you to learn English, too. There are many clubs at your school and in your community. Find the one that interests you.

Apply the Strategy

1. Ask your friends and classmates about campus clubs they belong to.

2. Ask about clubs at the information center on campus.

3. Look for clubs in your campus telephone book.

4. Look in the school newspaper for groups and organizations.

5. After you pick a club, attend a meeting. Ask questions about the club.

6. Get involved, meet people, and learn English!

PUTTING IT ALL TOGETHER

 **Find Someone Who . . .**

Practice talking about daily activities and using adverbs of frequency with all your classmates.

1. Stand up and walk around the room.

2. Ask each person a question. They should use an adverb of frequency to answer.

3. Write the person's name and answer in the blank.

4. Report what you learned to your class.

Most college campuses have a large number of student organizations to choose from. For example, at San Jose State University, a large urban university in Northern California, there are over 240 different clubs and organizations run by students.

EXAMPLE:

Susana is a morning person.

Jennifer and Erik sometimes run.

Julaine, Stefan, and Andy often ride their bikes.

Are you a night owl? _____

Are you a morning person? _____

Do you go to work at night? _____

Do you go to school at night? _____

Do you eat breakfast? _____

Do you skip lunch? _____

Do you ride your bike? _____

Do you run? _____

Do you play soccer? _____

Do you work at home? _____

Do you go to bed before ten? _____

Do you get up before six? _____

Do you play tennis? _____

Call an Automated Phone Service

Are there any automated phone services in English where you live? Ask your teacher. Call the phone service. Practice listening. Push buttons when instructed to. Have fun!

Listening for the Topic

A good way to practice listening for the topic is to spend time in a public place where people are talking in English. You can hear many different conversations. Good places to listen are in a café, on the bus, in the library, and on the elevator. If you are in a non-English-speaking country, practice listening for the topic by watching TV or films in English.

1. Listen to five different conversations. You do not need to see the people, just hear what they are saying.

2. Don't worry about hearing every detail. Just hear what you can.

3. Take notes.

4. Guess what they are talking about! For example:

   You hear, "Blah blah an iceberg. Blah blah blah Leonardo. Blah blah so sad. Blah blah romantic. Three hours long."

   You can guess that they are talking about the movie *Titanic*.

5. Report to your classmates what you heard.

Test-Taking Tip

Get a good night's sleep the night before the test. A solid night of sleep will help you think clearly. Sleep will also make you less likely to make silly mistakes. Try not to think about the test because it may make it difficult to fall asleep. Instead, before going to sleep, read a magazine or listen to some relaxing music.

CHECK YOUR PROGRESS

On a scale of 1 to 5, rate how well you have mastered the goals set at the beginning of the chapter:

1 2 3 4 5   talk about your regular schedule.

1 2 3 4 5   ask questions and participate in class.

1 2 3 4 5   use adverbs of frequency.

1 2 3 4 5   understand and pronounce sentence stress correctly.

1 2 3 4 5   listen for the topic of conversations.

1 2 3 4 5   start conversations with new people.

1 2 3 4 5   join a club or group on campus.

If you've given yourself a 3 or lower on any of these goals:

- visit the *Tapestry* web site for additional practice.
- ask your instructor for extra help.
- review the sections of the chapter that you found difficult.
- work with a partner or study group to further your progress.

L ook at the photo. Discuss these questions with your classmates:

- What is the weather like in this photo?
- How does the weather affect our lives?
- How many ways do you know to describe the weather?

idiom

IT'S RAINING CATS AND DOGS

One of the most famous American writers, Mark Twain, once said, "Everyone talks about the weather, but nobody does anything about it." Twain was making a joke. People talk about the weather because weather is considered a "safe" topic to talk about in the United States and Canada. It is safe because it is not controversial like other topics—for example, religion or politics. In this chapter, you will learn several different ways to talk and ask about weather. You will also learn about the natural forces that affect the weather. When you finish this chapter, you will be able to talk about the weather, but you still won't be able to do anything about it!

Setting Goals

In this chapter you will:

- talk about the weather.
- pronounce the /ng/ sound.
- use mental pictures to remember new words.
- ask questions about the weather.
- use a graphic organizer to understand and remember what you hear.
- learn to work and study well with others.
- participate in a group presentation.

◆ **Getting Started**

rain noun
raining verb
rainy adj

Look at the photos and pictures in this chapter. What do you already know about the different kinds of weather pictured in this chapter? What words are you unsure of? With your classmates, make a list of weather words that you already know.

PART 1: Talking About the Weather

·············

ice breaker
cold people

Talking about the weather is a good "ice breaker." When you just meet a person, talking about the weather is a good way to get a conversation going. You can say something like, "Wow, it's hot" or "What do you think about this weather?"

◆ **Getting Ready to Listen**

Look at the photos below. What kind of weather is in each photo? Work with a partner to describe the weather you see.

◆ **Listen**

Listening 1: Talking About the Weather

Listen to the people talk about the weather. Listen again and match the photo to the conversation.

snow and sleet

Poncho

burn off

it's a rainy day?

◆ **After You Listen**

Compare your answers with another student. Tell your partner which words or phrases helped you to make your decision. Discuss this question: Do you need to know what every word means to be able to understand what people are saying?

The United States is one of the few countries in the world that still uses the Fahrenheit scale to measure temperature. Canada and most other countries use the Celsius scale.

Thermometer

32° degree(s)
only time 1° degree

LANGUAGE YOU CAN USE:
TALKING ABOUT THE WEATHER

●●●

Here are some of the patterns you can use when talking about the weather:

1. It's snowing.
2. It's a snowy day.
3. It snows in the winter.
4. There's snow on the ground.
5. Snow is cold.
6. It's 5 degrees below zero.
7. The weather is cold.
8. It's freezing.

Notice that the first five sentences have a form of the word *snow* in it. Which sentences use *snow* as a verb? Which sentences use *snow* as a noun? Which sentence uses *snow* as an adjective?

USING NEW LANGUAGE

[handwritten margin notes:]
lighting (beautiful lighting in your house)
lightning
lightening
punyng te.

Make a sentence with each of these weather words. Practice saying the sentences to yourself. Then say the sentences with a partner.

rain	dry	sunny	thundering	85 degrees
rainy	cool	hot	raining	cloudy
windy	stormy	cold	warm	freezing

> "Red sky at night, sailors' delight; red sky in the morning, sailors take warning." This is a rhyme that sailors used to predict the weather before modern weather forecasting. It means a red sunset will be followed by a nice day and a red sunrise will be followed by a stormy day.

Note: Thunder and lightning happen during an electric storm. Thunder is the noise, and lightning is what you see. Both words are nouns.

Did your partner use any of the words differently than you? Look at the sample sentences again. Can you figure out the correct way to use the words? Check your sentences with your teacher. Can you make any rules about what kinds of words are used in different model sentences?

Talk About It

Look at the photos on page 80 again. Think of different ways to describe the weather in each photo. Work with a partner. Take turns describing the weather in the photos. Say at least five different things about each photo. Use affirmative and negative sentences. For example, you might describe the last photo this way:

- "It's a hot day."
- "It's not cold."
- "It isn't raining."
- "The weather is beautiful."
- "It's not too windy."

Now look at the weather outside your classroom. With your classmates, describe the weather outside in as many different ways as you can.

The Sound of It: The /ng/ Sound

The /ng/ sound that comes at the end of words like *raining, bang,* and *sing* is a little different than the /n/ sound that comes at the end of *rain, ban,* and *sin.* Listen to your teacher pronounce each of these pairs of words:

ping	pin
raining	rain
bang	ban
sung	sun
long	lawn
tongue	ton
sing	sin

Can you hear the difference between the two sounds? Practice saying the pairs of words. Do you sound like your teacher?

Sing

One way to practice a difficult sound is to sing songs or say rhymes that have the difficult sounds. Here are two rhymes that will help you with the /ng/ sound. Listen to this famous children's song. Play the tape again. Sing or say the words.

It's Raining. It's Pouring.

It's raining. It's pouring.
The old man is snoring.
He bumped his head and went to bed.
And couldn't get up in the morning.

◆ Rhyme

Here's another rhyme to practice:

> ### A Wet Day!
> • • • • • • • • • • • • •
>
> The rain is pouring, pouring, pouring.
> The rain is pouring; it's a rainy, rainy day.
> The wind is blowing, blowing, blowing.
> The wind is blowing; it's a windy, windy day.
> I am splashing, splashing, splashing.
> I am splashing through the puddles on my way.
> If the sun were shining, shining, shining.
> If the sun were shining, I wouldn't be wet today.

Now, if you want a real challenge, try to make your own rhyme to practice the /ng/ sound.

◆ Getting Ready to Listen

Look at this weather map. Find Ontario, Quebec, Ottawa, Vancouver, and Nova Scotia on the map. Then listen to the weather report.

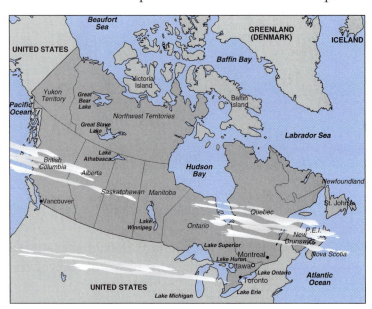

◆ Listen

Listening 2: A Weather Report

Listen to the weather report several times. Check the statements that are true.

_____ It is raining in Ottawa.

_____ The weather in Ottawa is terrible.

_____ It is spring.

_____ It is going to rain in Vancouver.

_____ It is very hot in Ottawa.

_____ It will rain a lot in Nova Scotia.

◆ After You Listen

Do you ever listen to weather reports in English on the radio or TV? This is a good way to practice your English skills. Try to listen to a radio or TV weather report in English at least two times this week. Write down any new vocabulary that you learn.

PART 2: How's the Weather?

Weather is a powerful force in nature. It is important to be able to ask about the weather. In this section, you will learn how to ask questions about the weather.

LANGUAGE LEARNING STRATEGY

To remember new vocabulary words, think about a picture that reminds you of the word. When you want to remember the word, just remember the picture. For example, if you want to learn the word *snowflake,* look at or draw a picture of a snowflake. Then close your eyes and remember the picture while you say the word. When you want to remember the word again, think about the picture.

Apply the Strategy

Look at these pictures of different kinds of weather and say the new word. Close your eyes and remember the picture and say the word again.

1. **Calm** weather means no wind.

2. A **breeze** is a slight wind. It's a breezy day.

tempraug

3. A **gust** is a sudden strong wind. The wind is gusting.

4. A **gale** is a strong windstorm. The gale sent the sailboat out to sea.

5. **Fog** is a cloud that comes down to the ground. It's foggy this morning.

6. **Overcast** means the clouds are hiding the sun. It's an overcast day.

marine layer

part cloud part sun

7. **Partly cloudy** means some clouds and some sun.

≠ partly suny

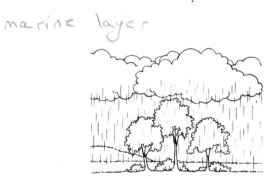

8. **Drizzle** means a little rain. It's drizzling.

a little rain

9. A **shower** is rain that begins and ends in a short time.

10. A **downpour** is a heavy rain.

long time

Now work with a partner. Take turns with your partner asking the meaning of the key words. For example:

Ling: "What does **drizzle** mean?"
Natalia: "**Drizzle** means a little rain."

LANGUAGE YOU CAN USE:
ASKING ABOUT THE WEATHER

Here are some ways to ask about the weather in English:

- How's the weather?
- What's the weather like today?
- What kind of day is it today?
- What do you think about this weather?
- It sure is hot, isn't it?

USING NEW LANGUAGE

Work with a partner. Cover up the words on page 86. Take turns with your partner asking about the weather. Example:

Alexi: How's the weather? (Point to picture #8.)
Andy: It's drizzling.
Alexi: What do you think about the weather today?
Andy: I don't like it. We have to stay inside all day when it rains.

Making Mental Pictures

You can use mental pictures even if you do not have photos of the new word. Another way to learn a new word is to draw a simple picture of the word you want to learn. You can write the word on a note card and draw the picture on the back of the note card. Look at the picture side of the note card and try to remember the word. For example, you might remember the word *lightning* like this:

lightning

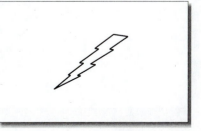

If you want to remember the word *lightning*, think of the picture.

Here are some more weather words. If you don't know the meaning of these words, look them up in a bilingual dictionary. Then make picture cards for the words. Work with a partner. Practice using the words in sentences. Your partner will show you the picture side of the card. You say a sentence that goes with each picture.

1. flood ~~on control~~ a lot of water
2. mudslide
3. avalanche *so much snow can kill you in mountain when active come down*
4. drought *no water*
5. raindrop *one drop of water*
6. tornado *siclone*
7. hurricane *not so rany bring win*
8. blizzard *only snow it's very windy & degree*
9. sleet *rain and snow it's ugly*
10. hail *Frozen rain drops*
11. snowflake
12. snow flurry *really light*
13. snow bank *snow*
14. blanket of snow *all the ground white*
15. rainbow
16. puddle *small water on grass*
17. dew *in the morning it doesn't rain (plants are wet)*
18. frost *Plants are crunchy*
19. humid
20. smog *polioution smog + fog*

Think About It

Compare your drawings to your partner's drawings. Talk about how they are different and similar. Do you think it is easier to remember new words when you look at a picture? Do you think it is easier to remember new words if you draw your own picture? Do you think it is easier to remember new words by looking at your partner's picture? Explain your answers.

There are several idioms in the United States about the weather. For example, "It's raining cats and dogs" means it is raining very hard. When it is rainy and wet all day, people may say, "It's a day for the ducks." You can remember these idioms by remembering these funny pictures:

image of dew

You can see a rainbow when there is sunshine and rain at the same time. Rainbows are the reflection of sun on raindrops. Rainbows are curved because raindrops are round. Rainbow colors are always in the same order: red, orange, yellow, green, blue, indigo, and violet.

◀ Talk About It

Snowflakes are made of ice crystals. They all have six sides, but no two snowflakes are exactly the same.

Think about the weather patterns in your native country. What is the weather like in the summer, winter, spring, and fall? Do you come from a country that has a wet and a dry season? Tell a partner six things about the weather in your native country. Listen while your partner tells you something about the weather in his or her native country. Examples:

- In the spring there is a lot of thunder and lightning in the United States.
- Canada is snowy in the winter.
- It's humid in the wet season in Brazil.
- In India, it seldom rains in the dry season.
- In Japan, it snows in the mountains in the winter.
- There are typhoons in Taiwan in the wet season.

What did you learn about the weather in your partner's native country?

Culture Note

Smog is a word used to describe air pollution in the United States and Canada. It is a fairly new word in the English language. It was created by combining the words *smoke* and *fog*.

LANGUAGE LEARNING STRATEGY

Use a graphic organizer to understand and remember what you hear. Look at the chart on the next page. This kind of chart is called a **graphic organizer**. Graphic organizers connect words by their meaning. A graphic organizer shows the connections between words and ideas. Graphic organizers can help you in many ways:

- They can help you understand what you hear.
- They can help you remember vocabulary words.

(continued on next page)

- They can help you take better notes about what you read and hear.

- They can help you plan your ideas when you write.

- They can help you remember what to say when you have to give an oral presentation.

Apply the Strategy

What words do you already know to describe the weather? Work with a partner. Finish this graphic organizer with as many words as you know about the weather. Don't worry if you don't fill in all the circles; just try to think of as many as you can.

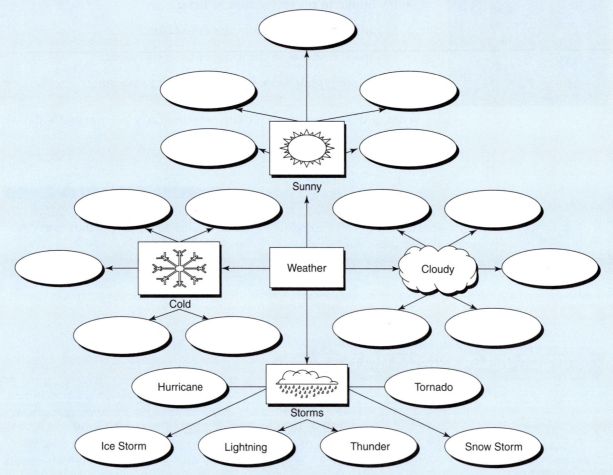

After you finish the chart, your teacher will help you compare your chart with the other students in the class. Make a class chart with all of the students' ideas. (Expand the chart and make more circles if you need them.) Did you learn some new weather words from your classmates? How did the graphic organizer help you understand the meaning of new words that you heard?

Talk About It

There is no one way to organize information. For example, you could organize the new weather words you have learned by the kind of sentence they are in.

Work with a partner. Look at this graphic organizer. Discuss how it is organized. Finish this graphic organizer.

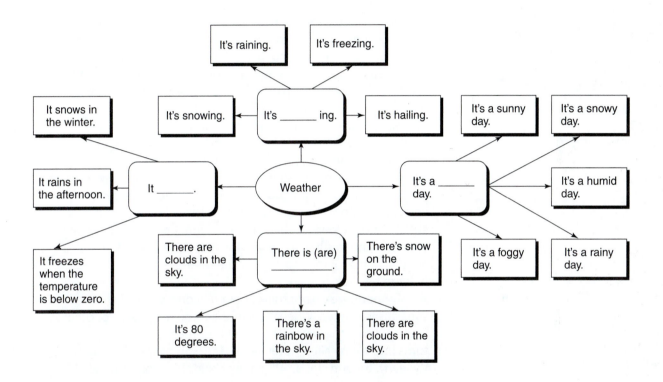

Compare this graphic organizer with the first one you completed. How are they similar? How are they different? How do the pictures help you remember new words?

Getting Ready to Read

Skim the reading text. Match the main ideas with each paragraph.

_____ The sun controls the weather in different parts of the world.

_____ The sun causes rain and other precipitation.

_____ The sun causes all kinds of weather.

_____ The sun causes wind.

Read

As you read this selection about the weather, look at the pictures. The pictures will help you understand the text.

The Power of the Sun

1 Without the sun, there would be no weather. Light from the sun not only causes sunny days, but it also causes weather to be different in different parts of the world. The sun causes all other kinds of weather, including wind, rain, and even snow.

2 Weather is different in different parts of the world because the sun shines brightest on the parts of the world that are closest to the sun. The earth is shaped like a ball. The part of the earth that is nearest to the sun is near the equator, the fattest part of the ball. That means the part of the earth nearest the equator is the warmest and air at the North and South Poles is the coldest. You might think that the sun would make the mountains very warm because mountains are high in the air. However, at high elevations the air is very thin. It cannot hold the warmth of the sun like air at lower elevations.

3 The sun causes wind too. Warm air moves towards cooler air, and cool air moves towards warmer air. The warm air near the equator moves towards the north and south poles. Cool air from the north and south poles moves towards the equator. Wind is another name for this moving air. The wind can be a light breeze, or it can be a strong gale.

4 Although we do not think about rain on a sunny day, the sun causes rain too. When the sun shines on the oceans or other water, it heats the water. The water becomes so warm that it turns into a gas called water vapor. The water vapor rises from the earth to form clouds. When the clouds hit cooler air, the

The hottest place in the world is Dallol, Ethiopia. Annual temperatures average 94 degrees F (34 degrees C).

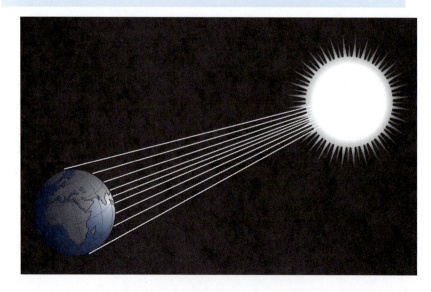

water vapor turns into liquid again. The water vapor falls to the ground in raindrops. If the air is really cold, the water vapor turns into snow or hail.

5   So the next time it is a rainy or stormy day, remember that both good weather and bad weather are caused by the sun.

◆ **After You Read**

After you have read "The Power of the Sun," complete the graphic organizer on the next page. This will help you organize the information to better understand what you have read. Add more groups if you need them.

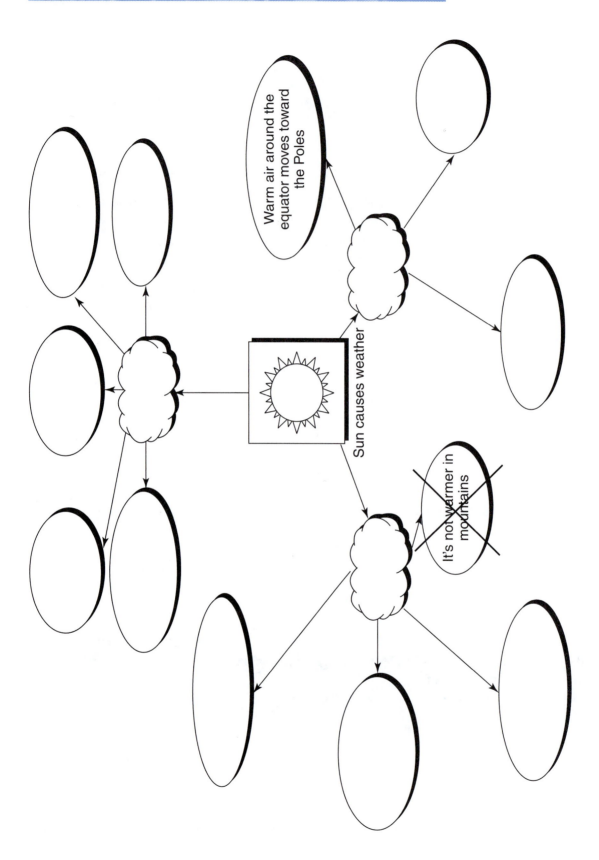

Vocabulary Building   Did you understand all of the words in "The Power of the Sun"? Check your understanding of the vocabulary by doing the crossword puzzle below.

Across

3. Water vapor turns into _____ when it falls to the earth.

4. The sun _____ weather to be different in different parts of the world.

8. The middle of the earth is called the _____.

10. A soft, gentle wind is called a _____.

12. A strong wind is called a _____.

14. If something is not solid or gas, it's _____.

15. Everest is an example of a _____.

Down

1. The sun shines _____ at the equator.

2. North and South _____.

5. How's the _____ today?

6. There is only one _____ in the sky.

7. The _____ of the sun.

9. Mountains have higher _____ than the sea.

11. Frozen raindrops are called _____.

13. Clouds are made of water _____.

PART 3: Weather Report

Scientists who study the weather are called meteorologists. Some meteorologists also report about the weather on radio or TV. Meteorologists also predict what the weather will be like in the near future. This prediction is called the weather forecast.

Talking About Global Warming

Did you know that the weather is getting hotter each year? Scientists call this trend "global warming." People cause global warming. Pollution from cars and factories causes warm air to stay near the earth. This means the earth gets hotter and hotter.

The video you will watch is about global warming. Look at the photos that go with the video. Before you watch the video, discuss these questions with your classmates:

1. What do you see in the photos?

2. What do you know about global warming already?

3. How do you think global warming affects the weather?

4. What do you think you will learn from the video?

As you watch the video, think about the class discussion.

TUNING IN: "Global Warming"

Watch the video. Don't try to understand everything. Just get the main idea of what the video is about. Watch the video again. As you watch, finish writing the main ideas in the following graphic organizer. The first one has been done for you as an example. After you watch the video, compare your graphic organizer with your partner's graphic organizer. How are they similar or different?

© CNN

© CNN

Groundhog Day is February 2 in the United States. People say that if the groundhog sees his shadow on that day, the weather will be cold for six more weeks.

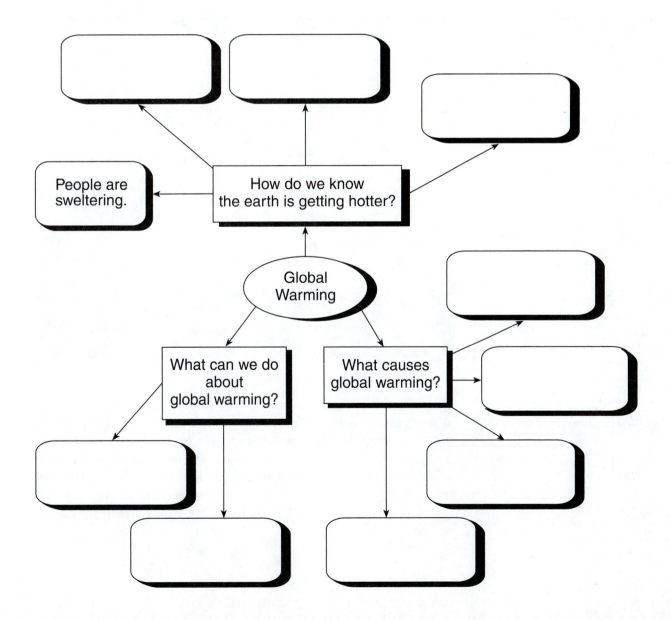

People are sweltering.

How do we know the earth is getting hotter?

Global Warming

What can we do about global warming?

What causes global warming?

◆Idea Exchange

With your classmates, discuss solutions to the problem of global warming. How can we reduce pollution? How can we convince people that it is important to control global warming?

ACADEMIC POWER STRATEGY

Learn to work and study well with other students. This can help you learn more and understand what you are studying better. Teachers often require students to work together in pairs or small groups. When all members participate, group work can be fun and successful. However, if one person does all of the work or takes control of the group, it can be an unpleasant experience. In the same way, if one person does not participate, the group experience can be negative.

You will be given steps to follow. Follow all of these steps as you do this group activity. You will find that you practice English and learn a lot. Even if your teacher does not require you to do group work, studying with a group of students can help you learn better. Don't be shy. Ask some of your classmates if they would like to study with you.

Apply the Strategy

Consider the following questions carefully. Write short answers to the questions. Your teacher will help you form groups so that you can talk about what makes a good group experience.

Questionnaire

1. Are you a shy person or an outgoing person? Explain why you are shy or outgoing.

2. Did you ever study for a test with a group of students before? If the answer is "yes," tell what test you studied for and how the group studied.

3. Did you ever work on a project with a group of students before? If the answer is "yes," explain the project.

4. Was it a successful or unpleasant group experience? Explain.

5. What are three things that good group members do?

When you meet with your group, follow these steps:

1. Arrange your desks or chairs so that you are facing each other in a circle.

2. Go around the circle and introduce yourselves. Make sure you know the name of each member of your group.

3. Three members of the group will have a group role. Read about the roles and choose a group member for each role.

(continued on next page)

> ### Roles
>
> **Facilitator:** The facilitator makes sure each group member speaks for the same amount of time. He or she makes sure all the group members are heard.
>
> **Recorder:** The recorder takes notes on what the group members say.
>
> **Summarizer:** The summarizer uses the notes the recorder takes. He or she tells the whole class what the group discussed.

4. Tell the group members about what you wrote in the questionnaire.

5. Listen to the members of your group as they tell about their experiences.

6. After each member of your group has had a chance to speak, look at the notes. Decide what things you would like to share with all of your classmates. The summarizer will tell all your classmates about one bad group experience and one successful group experience. Share your list of qualities of a good group member.

◆ Working in Groups

As you do this small group activity, remember your discussion about what makes a successful group experience. You will work with a group of students to do a TV weather report. With your group:

1. Decide what region you would like to report on the weather. (It can be anywhere—your city, somewhere in South America, Asia, Europe, Africa, or even Antarctica.)

2. Find out about the weather in the place you choose by watching TV news, looking in books or newspapers, or searching on the internet. You can also watch the *Global Warming* video again to get some ideas on how to give a weather report.

3. Create a 3- to 5-minute weather report. All group members should talk during the weather report.

4. Create a visual aid like a map or chart that goes along with the oral presentation.

5. Practice how you will make the presentation to your classmates.

Some Tips for Each Speaker

- Do not read or memorize your presentation. Just talk as though you were having a conversation.
- Practice your part of the presentation in front of a mirror. This will help you know how you look when you talk.
- Talk in a loud voice. Listen to the presentation of each group member to make sure that his or her voice is loud and clear.
- R–E–L–A–X. Remember that you are going to make this presentation for your classmates. They are all learning English too.
- If you make a mistake, don't worry. Just continue with your part of the presentation. Everyone makes mistakes.

Some Tips for the Group

- Make sure there is a smooth transition between speakers.
- Listen to the other members of the group as they practice their part of the weather report.
- Give other members of the group advice on how they can make their part better.
- Time the whole presentation to make sure it is at least 3 minutes long.
- Check your map or chart to make sure the grammar and spelling are correct.

After you complete this group project, write the answers to these questions using complete sentences.

Write About It.

GROUP PROJECT–EVALUATION FORM

1. What was the best thing about the group project?

_____

_____

_____

_____

_____

2. What is one thing I would like to change about the group project?

_____

_____

_____

_____

_____

3. What did I do to help the group?

_____

_____

_____

_____

_____

4. Explain one thing you learned from a group member.

_____

_____

_____

_____

_____

5. Explain one thing you learned by doing this project.

_____

_____

_____

_____

_____

PUTTING IT ALL TOGETHER

Your teacher may assign one or all of the activities below.

 **Organized Geography**

1. Work with a partner to finish the graphic organizer on the next page about geographical features. Use a bilingual dictionary to help find words you are not sure of.

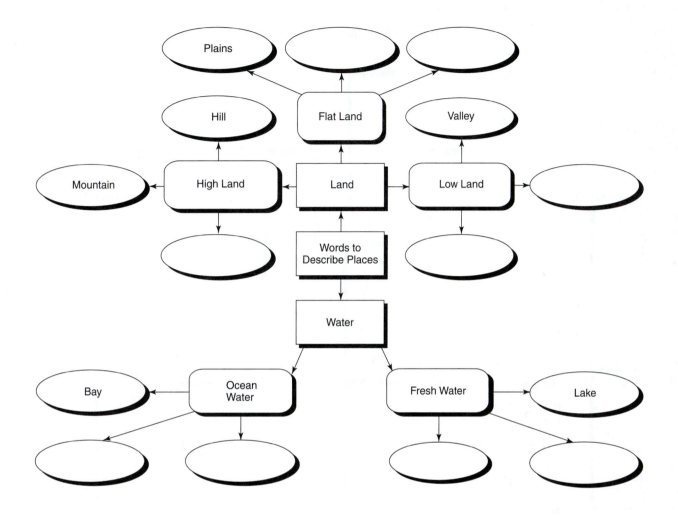

2. Make pictures to go with the words on your graphic organizer.

More Group Presentations   Do a group presentation. Make a graphic organizer or illustrations to go with your presentation. Here are some suggested topics. Your teacher may want to add more.

tornadoes	typhoons
El Niño	thunderstorms
droughts	global warming
blizzards	hurricanes
La Niña	floods
avalanches	tropical weather

Here is an example:

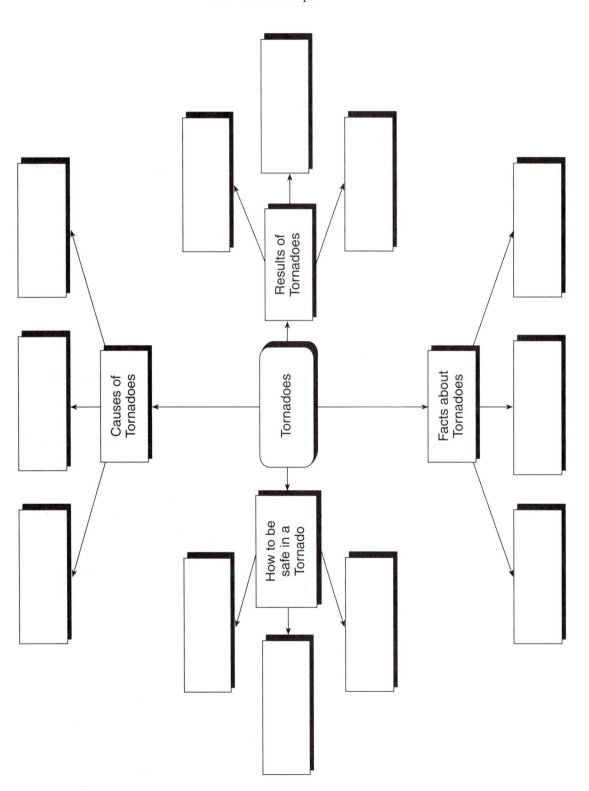

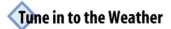 **Tune in to the Weather**

Look at and/or listen to weather reports on TV, in newspapers, on the radio, or on the Internet. Compare the different reports. Tell how they are similar and different.

Test-Taking Tip

The night before the test, gather the things you need to have with you at the test, including pens, pencils, erasers, a watch, etc. You may also need tissues, cough drops, etc. Coming to the test with everything you need will ensure that you won't worry about these details during the test.

CHECK YOUR PROGRESS

On a scale of 1 to 5, rate how well you have mastered the goals set at the beginning of the chapter:

1 2 3 4 5   talk about the weather.

1 2 3 4 5   pronounce the /ng/ sound.

1 2 3 4 5   use mental pictures to remember new words.

1 2 3 4 5   ask questions about the weather.

1 2 3 4 5   use a graphic organizer to understand and remember what you hear.

1 2 3 4 5   learn to work and study well with others.

1 2 3 4 5   participate in a group presentation.

If you've given yourself a 3 or lower on any of these goals:

- visit the *Tapestry* web site for additional practice.

- ask your instructor for extra help.

- review the sections of the chapter that you found difficult.

- work with a partner or study group to further your progress.

Discuss these questions in a small group:

- What are these people doing?
- What do you think they're saying?
- In your native culture, do you do or say anything before you begin to eat? If you do say something, what does it mean in English?
- Look at the title of the chapter. What does "To Your Health" mean?

TO YOUR HEALTH

In this chapter, you will learn about matters related to health. You will talk about being sick and getting well. You will also learn about visiting the doctor. Finally, you will hear information about ways to stay healthy. To your health!

Setting Goals

In this chapter you will learn to:

- ◆ describe your symptoms.
- ◆ understand and give advice.
- ◆ know when to give strong advice and when to make suggestions.
- ◆ practice telephone conversations before you call.
- ◆ listen for sequence words and phrases.
- ◆ pronounce /th/ correctly.
- ◆ find healthy ways to reduce stress.

"To your health!" is a special expression called a *toast*. A toast is something you say at a special event. We make a toast before eating a special meal, during a holiday, or at a wedding. Many languages have a similar expression. For example, in Hebrew people say, "L'chaim!" In French, people say, "A votre sante!" In Italian, they say, "Cin Cin!" In Japanese, they say, "Kam Pai!" In English, we also say, "Cheers!" They all have a similar meaning. What do you say in your first language?

Getting Started

All languages have proverbs (traditional expressions about life and how to live). Look at these proverbs. What do they say about health and how to live a healthy life? Discuss them in a small group.

- An apple a day keeps the doctor away.
- You are what you eat.
- I would rather be healthy than rich.
- To be happy is to be healthy.

PART 1: Being Sick

It is important to be able to talk about health problems so you can get advice and help from a doctor. When we talk about our health, we talk about *symptoms*. Symptoms are signs of sickness. For example, if you have a fever and a cough, you might have the flu. A fever and a cough are symptoms. When you are sick, you must describe your symptoms to a doctor or other health-care worker.

Common Symptoms

Work with a partner. Read the list of symptoms and look at the pictures. Then write the name of the correct symptom under each

> Health is a state of complete physical, mental and social well-being, and not merely the absence of disease or infirmity.
>
> **—THE WORLD HEALTH ORGANIZATION**

picture. If there is a symptom you are not familiar with, look it up in a dictionary or ask your teacher.

a fever	a backache
a stuffy nose	a rash
a headache	a twisted ankle
a cough	a stomachache
a sore throat	a stiff neck

_____

_____

_____

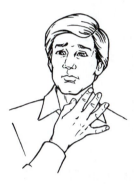

_____

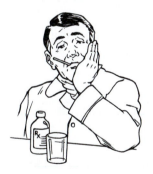

_____

_____

_____

_____

_____

_____

LANGUAGE YOU CAN USE: DESCRIBING SYMPTOMS

EXPRESSIONS

I have a _____.

I feel _____.

My _____ hurts.

EXAMPLES

I have a stuffy nose.

I have a sore throat.

I feel dizzy.

I feel sick to my stomach.

My arm hurts.

My back hurts.

USING NEW LANGUAGE

> **Studies of stress show a clear relationship between stress and self-reported colds and influenza.**
>
> **—COHEN & WILLIAMSON**

Practice the new language with a partner. Take turns asking about your health and describing your symptoms.

A: What's the matter?

B: _____

A: How are you feeling?

B: _____

A: What's wrong?

B: _____

A: Are you feeling all right?

B: _____

A: Are you sick?

B: _____

 Charades

In a group of four or five, take turns acting out the symptoms on the next page. Remember not to speak! The members of your group should guess what the problem is.

a fever   a backache

a stuffy nose   a rash

a headache   a stomachache

a cough   a stiff neck

a sore throat   other symptoms that you know!

◀Getting Ready to Listen   Before you listen, learn some helpful vocabulary. Read the sentences below. Then try to guess the meaning of the underlined words and expressions.

1. My friend likes to go to the <u>climbing gym</u> to exercise. I don't like to climb because I am afraid of falling.

2. Every Sunday, I go to yoga class and practice <u>stretching</u> my body.

3. If you are sick, you might want to take some <u>medicine</u> such as aspirin.

4. If you have a rash on your arms or legs, you might have <u>poison oak</u>.

5. If you have poison oak, you will feel very <u>itchy</u>.

6. If you have a rash, you should try not to <u>scratch</u> it.

Now draw a line between the word or expression and the picture that shows the meaning. The first one has been done for you.

a climbing gym

to stretch

medicine

poison oak

to scratch

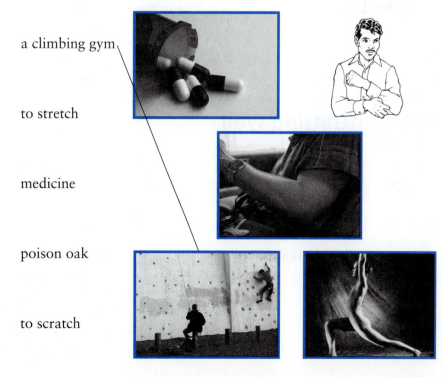

Listen

Listening 1: Talking About Symptoms

Listen to the first three conversations. Check off all the symptoms you hear. You may hear more than one symptom for each.

CONVERSATION ONE

_____ a backache

_____ a stomachache

_____ a headache

_____ a toothache

CONVERSATION TWO

_____ a sore throat

_____ a sore back

_____ a stiff neck

_____ a twisted ankle

CONVERSATION THREE

_____ a stuffy nose

_____ a cough

_____ a fever

_____ a rash

Now listen to the next three conversations. Fill in the blanks with the symptoms you hear.

CONVERSATION FOUR

She has a _____ .

She feels _____ .

CONVERSATION FIVE

His _____ hurts.

He feels _____ .

CONVERSATION SIX

Mary and Doug have a _____ .

They feel _____ .

 **After You Listen**

Work with a partner. Discuss these questions.

1. Have you had any of these symptoms? When?

2. What did you do to get well?

PART 2: Getting Well

When you are sick, people often offer their advice on how to get well. You can get advice from your friends, your family, and your doctor.

Getting Ready to Listen

Hiro is a student who has a health problem. He has a lot of stress in his life and gets sick very often. You will hear advice from three people who want to help him. Before you listen, try to predict what you will hear. Write down three suggestions for how Hiro can reduce, or lessen, his stress and improve his health.

1. _____
2. _____
3. _____

 Listen

Listening 2: Giving Advice

Listen to the conversations. What advice does each speaker give to Hiro? Write each person's advice on the lines below.

His friend:

You could _____

His mother:

You should _____

His doctor:

You have to _____

The average number of visits to the doctor per person per year in the United States: 3.4.

 After You Listen

Discuss these questions with a classmate:

1. What do you think about the advice that Hiro gets?

2. Who gave the best advice? Why?

LANGUAGE YOU CAN USE: GIVING ADVICE

There are several ways to give advice in English. Some ways are very strong. Other ways are not as strong. It's important to know when to give strong advice and when to make a suggestion. In the United States and Canada for example, you can give strong advice to a close friend or family member. You should not give strong advice to your boss or your teacher. Instead, you should make a suggestion.

Suggestion	Example
You could . . .	You could drink orange juice.
You should/ought to . . .	You ought to exercise more.
	You should go to sleep early.

Strong Advice	Example
You had better . . .*	You had better see a doctor.
You must . . .	You must take some medicine.

You had better is pronounced *you'd better* in speaking.

◈Strong Advice or Suggestion?

It is important to think about your relationship to people when giving advice. Look at the list of people below. In each case, is it appropriate or acceptable to offer strong advice? Or is it better to make a suggestion? Write *A* for strong advice and *S* for suggestion.

_____ 1. Student to teacher

_____ 2. Doctor to patient

_____ 3. Close friend to close friend

_____ 4. Co-worker to co-worker

_____ 5. Parents to children

_____ 6. Grandson to grandmother

_____ 7. Professor to student

_____ 8. Businessperson to supervisor

_____ 9. Salesperson to customer

_____10. Boss to employee

USING NEW LANGUAGE
●●●

Practice making suggestions or giving advice. Work with a partner. Partner A should make a sentence using the problem on the left. Partner B should make a suggestion or give advice using the expression on the right. Example:

(sore throat)   You should . . .

I have a bad sore throat.   You should drink tea with honey.

1. (bad cold)   You could . . .

2. (no time to exercise)   You should . . .

3. (want to stop smoking)   You must . . .

Now Partner B will make a sentence using the problem on the left. Partner A will make a suggestion or give advice using the expression on the right.

4. (too much stress)   You ought to . . .

5. (want to eat better)   You could . . .

6. (need more sleep)   You must . . .

Find the Best Advice

1. Think of another health problem like the ones in the last activity. Write it down on a small piece of paper.

2. Now get up and tell at least four people about your problem. They should give you advice.

3. When you are finished, decide who gave you the best advice. Give that person the small piece of paper with your problem written on it.

4. Find out who has the most pieces of paper. This person is the winner. You should probably ask him or her for advice the next time you have a problem!

Getting Ready to Listen

You will hear a patient telephone a doctor's office to make an appointment. An *appointment* is a scheduled meeting time. Before you listen, predict what questions the receptionist in the doctor's office will ask. Make a list of questions.

Questions:

A. What seems to be the problem?

B. _____

C. _____

D. _____

Listen

Listening 3: Making an Appointment

Listen to the telephone conversation. Circle the correct answer.

1. The caller wants

    a. to make an appointment.

    b. to ask for advice.

2. The caller wants to see the doctor because

    a. she is sick.

    b. she wants a checkup.

3. The caller makes an appointment

    a. for Tuesday.

    b. for Thursday.

4. The caller's appointment is

    a. at 4:15.

    b. at 4:50.

Now listen again. Fill in the missing words and phrases. You might need to listen several times.

> Susan: Hello. Doctor Basso's office. This is Susan. May I help you?
>
> Ms. Kim: Hello. This is So-Young Kim. I'd like _____
>
> _____ with Dr. Basso.
>
> Susan: What seems to be the problem, Ms. Kim?
>
> Ms. Kim: Actually, I'm _____ sick. I'd like _____
>
> for my yearly checkup.
>
> Susan: OK, fine. Dr. Basso has some time next Thursday. Is that day
>
> good for you?
>
> Ms. Kim: Let me see. _____. Actually, Thursday
>
> isn't good for me. _____ the following Tuesday?
>
> Susan: Yes. We have openings on Tuesday. How about Tuesday then?
>
> Ms. Kim: Yeah. Tuesday would be just fine. _____?
>
> Susan: We have an opening at 4:15.
>
> Ms. Kim: _____ sounds good.

Susan: OK. Can you spell your name?

Ms. Kim: Kim. K-I-M. First name So-Young. S-O Y-O-U-N-G.

Susan: All right, Ms. Kim. We have you scheduled to come in next Tuesday, March 17 at 4:15. You'll see Dr. Basso for a checkup. Is that correct?

Ms. Kim: Yes. _____.

Susan: You're welcome. See you next Tuesday.

Ms. Kim: _____ Tuesday.

After You Listen

Discuss these questions with a partner:

1. What is a checkup? Ask your partner to explain if you do not know.

2. Do you visit the doctor every year? Why or why not?

3. Have you ever made an appointment over the phone in English? If so, was it difficult or easy? Tell your partner about it.

LANGUAGE LEARNING STRATEGY

Practice telephone conversations before you call. Talking on the phone can be very difficult. You can't see faces or gestures to help you understand. Practicing the conversation first will help you to prepare what to say. It will also help you to predict what the other person will say. Finally, practicing will help you feel more relaxed when you make the call. You will understand more and express yourself easily when you call! There are three steps to follow:

1. Predict what the other person will say and ask.

2. Practice what you will say. You might want to practice with a friend.

3. Make the telephone call!

Apply the Strategy

Work with a partner. One of you is partner A. The other is partner B.

1. Partner A, pretend that you are sick and need to make an appointment with the doctor. Think about what you will say.

(continued on next page)

2. Partner B, you will answer the phone in the doctor's office. Think about what you will say.

3. Now practice the telephone conversation several times.

4. Switch roles. Partner B is the patient, and partner A will answer the phone.

5. Your teacher may ask you to present one of your conversations to your classmates.

Culture Note

Visiting the doctor can be confusing. Often, you must wait a long time to see the doctor. When you finally see the doctor, it is often just for a short time, so it's important to be prepared to speak to the doctor and to understand what the doctor tells you.

STUDENT HEALTH CENTER
San Jose State University

Health Building - Room 106
(Corner, 9th & Paseo de San Carlos)
(408) 924-6120
http://www.sjsu.edu/depts/
Student_Health/homepage.html

◆ **Getting Ready to Listen**

You will listen to a conversation between a student and a doctor in the Student Health Center. Before you listen, work in a small group and answer these questions:

1. What are some common health problems for students? Write them here.

_____

_____

_____

2. Do you think students get sick more often or less often than other people? Why?

◆ **Listen**

Listening 4: Talking to a Doctor

Part 1 Listen to the beginning of the student's visit. Check off the health problem you hear:

_____ The student has the flu.

_____ The student has trouble sleeping.

_____ The student has a bad cold.

Part 2 You will now hear the rest of the visit. The doctor will advise the patient to do three things. Listen for his advice and write it here:

1. _____

2. _____

3. _____

After You Listen

Discuss these questions with a partner.

1. Do you think the doctor gave good advice? Why or why not?

2. What advice would you give the patient?

3. Have you ever had a similar problem? If yes, what did you do?

Role Play

Work with a partner. Practice talking to a doctor and giving advice. One student should be a patient and describe some symptoms. The other student should be the doctor and give some advice.

PART 3: Staying Healthy

Getting Ready to Read

You are going to read about the benefits, or good effects, of exercise. Before you read, try to brainstorm as many good effects of exercise as you can in five minutes. Write them here:

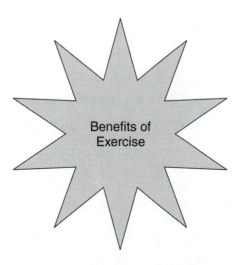

Benefits of
Exercise

Read

As you read, think about your predictions. How many of the benefits that you brainstormed are in the reading?

1 Everyone knows that exercise is good for you **physically.** Exercise helps you to lose weight. It also helps you to maintain a healthy body weight. Exercise can help to prevent diseases such as heart disease and cancer. Exercising every day keeps your body fit and strong.

2   But did you also know that exercise is good for you **psychologically?** It's true! Here are some ways that exercise helps your brain, mind, and spirit:

- Exercise helps you to think more clearly.
- Exercise helps reduce **tension** and **stress.**
- Exercise makes you feel better about yourself.
- Exercise makes problems feel smaller.
- Exercise helps you to be more **creative.**
- Exercise improves your **mood.**

3   You can see that there are a lot of **benefits** for your body *and* your mind and spirit. So why not exercise? You don't have to run a **marathon** to get these benefits. You could take a walk, play basketball, or ride a bike. Get off the couch and move your body every day. Your body will say, "Thank you!"

Vocabulary Building

Take the vocabulary quiz. Write *T* if the statement is true. Write *F* if the statement is false.

_____ 1. A **benefit** is a bad effect, or negative result, of doing something.

_____ 2. If something is good for you **physically,** it is good for your body.

_____ 3. If something is good for you **psychologically,** it is good for your mind and spirit.

_____ 4. **Tension** is different from stress.

_____ 5. If you are **creative,** you do not have any good, new ideas.

_____ 6. Your **mood** is your general feeling.

_____ 7. A **marathon** is a really long race.

After You Read

Based on the reading, when is a good time to exercise? Put a check mark next to the situations where exercise can help:

_____ When you want to study effectively.

_____ When you feel stress.

_____ When you feel depressed.

_____ When you have a problem.

_____ When you want to have good new ideas.

_____ When you feel bad.

Discuss these questions with a partner:

1. What new information did you learn about the benefits of exercise?

2. Will you change your exercise habits? Why or why not?

LANGUAGE LEARNING STRATEGY

Listen for sequence words and phrases to help you understand what you hear. When people are speaking, they often use sequence words and phrases such as *first, next,* and *finally*. These words can help you find and understand the important points in a lecture, a news report, or a conversation. If you don't pay attention to these words, you may miss some very important information. Sequence words also help you listen for the main ideas.

Here is a list of common sequence words. Can you add others?

Sequence Words and Phrases	Examples
First, . . .	*First,* you should exercise every day.
The first (second, next, last, etc.) benefit is . . .	*The first benefit* of exercise *is* weight loss.
Second, . . .	*Second,* you should eat more vegetables.
Third, . . .	*Third,* you must sleep at least seven hours.
Next, . . .	*Next,* you have to wear a seat belt.
My last (second, third, final, etc.) point is . . .	*My last point* is you ought to stop smoking.
Finally, . . .	*Finally,* you should try to have some fun every day.

Apply the Strategy

You will hear a short lecture on why people don't exercise. It is from a health telephone information line. Listen carefully for sequence words and phrases to understand the lecture.

Getting Ready to Listen

Do you think it is difficult to exercise often? Why or why not? Write your reason here.

_____

_____

Listen   **Listening 5: Exercise Information Line**

First Listening

Don't worry if you don't understand everything. Just listen for the sequence words and phrases. Write them on the left side of the chart. The first one has been done for you.

Second Listening

Listen for the reasons why people don't exercise. Write them on the right side of the chart. The first one has been done for you.

SEQUENCE WORDS AND PHRASES	REASONS WHY PEOPLE DON'T EXERCISE
1. "The first problem . . .	1. "No time."
2.	2.
3.	3.
4.	4.
5.	5.

Third Listening

Listen for the solutions. Draw a line from the reasons to the solutions. The first one has been done for you on the following page.

 **After You Listen**

Think about what you heard. Talk to a partner about these questions:

1. Go back to Getting Ready to Listen on p. 121. Look at what you wrote. Did you hear any of your reasons in the listening? Tell your partner.

2. Do you think you will try the solutions in the lecture? Why or why not?

(REASONS)   **(SOLUTIONS)**

| No time |

| No money |

| Too tired |

| Bad weather |

| Embarrassed |

You don't have to join a gym. Walk.

Exercise inside.

Exercise every day —it will give you energy.

Don't feel bad; you should feel great!

You should take two or three short walks every day.

 Snacking

Look at the cartoon below. Discuss this question with a partner:
   Why does the boy say that he and his mother are not speaking the same language?

Calvin and **Hobbes**   by **Bill Watterson**

© CNN

TUNING IN: "Snacking"

You will watch a video about snacking. You will learn about the most popular snacks in the United States. Before you watch, predict what the most popular snacks are. Put a check mark next to what you think are the three most popular snack items. Discuss your answers with a few classmates.

_____ ice cream   _____ tortilla chips

_____ raw carrots   _____ pretzels

_____ fruit   _____ cookies

_____ potato chips   _____ candy

Watch the first part of the report. Fill in the blanks.

> As millions and millions bite into snack foods, snack food companies are taking an impressive bite out of the American food dollar.
>
> _____ % of people in the USA snack at least
>
> _____ a day. So this is truly an American pastime.
> And as the insatiable number of snack food choices keep growing,
>
> people keep eating _____. And _____.
>
> And _____ than ever before.
>
> Last year, Americans spent _____ dollars on
>
> snack foods, and that equates to about _____ and a
>
> _____ pounds per person. And here's another statis-
>
> tic to swallow. More than _____ billion dollars'
>
> worth were crunched and munched in _____.

You will hear the results of a survey on Americans' eating habits. Watch the second part of the report and answer these questions:

1. What types of snacks are most popular?
   a. salty, crunchy snacks   b. sweet snacks

2. What is the most popular snack in the evening?
   a. potato chips   b. ice cream

3. What is the most popular time for a snack attack?

   a. in the afternoon   b. in the evening

4. What is the most popular snack in the United States?

   a. potato chips   b. pretzels

After you watch, discuss these questions:

1. What is your favorite snack? Why do you like it?

2. Is your favorite snack healthy or unhealthy?

3. What time of day do you usually want a snack?

 **Getting Ready to Listen** You will hear another short listening from a telephone information line. This lecture tells you how to stay healthy. With a partner, try to predict ways to stay healthy. Use the chart to predict what you will hear.

WHAT YOU *SHOULD* DO	WHAT YOU SHOULD *NOT* DO
"Exercise everyday."	"Drink a lot of alcohol."

 Listen

Listening 6: Staying Healthy

Don't worry if you can't understand everything. Just listen for the sequence words and phrases. Take notes on the ten ways to stay healthy. The first one has been done for you.

1. Exercise everyday.

2. _____

3. _____

4. _____

5. _____

6. _____

7. _____

8. _____

9. _____

10. _____

After You Listen

Look at the ten ways to stay healthy from the last activity. Put a check mark next to the advice you already follow in your life. Circle the things you don't do. Tell a classmate about what you do and don't do.

The Sound of It: Pronouncing the /th/ Sound

An important sound in English is /th/. In this chapter, you have seen and heard many words with the /th/ sound:

throat	I have a sore *throat*.
Thursday	My appointment is on *Thursday*.
three	Here are *three* suggestions to get well.
healthy	Eat vegetables for a *healthy* body.
fourth	My *fourth* suggestion is to exercise every day.

He had much experience of physicians, and said, "the only way to keep your health is to eat what you don't want, drink what you don't like, and do what you'd druther not."

—MARK TWAIN

Listen for /th/

Listen to the word pairs. Circle the word you hear.

1. thigh   sigh

2. thin   sin

3. throat   tote

4. three   tree

5. tenth   tense

6. mouth   mouse

Now listen to the last section of the lecture again. Fill in the missing words.

> You have heard ten ways to stay _____. We hope
>
> you will remember these and follow our advice. First, exercise
>
> every day. Second, get enough sleep. _____, eat
>
> green things. _____, don't smoke. _____,

don't drink a lot of alcohol. _____, wear a seat belt. _____, drink lots of water. _____, visit your doctor for regular checkups. _____, reduce stress. _____, spend time with friends and family.

Group Practice

Read these suggestions for staying healthy. Which do you think is most important? Which do you think is least important? Put them in order. Write *first, second, third, fourth,* or *fifth* next to each suggestion.

_____ A. Eat green things.

_____ B. Drink lots of water.

_____ C. Wear a seat belt.

_____ D. Don't smoke.

_____ E. Exercise every day.

Practice /th/ in a small group. Discuss your list of suggestions. For example, "I think _____ should be fourth because . . . ."

ACADEMIC POWER STRATEGY

Find healthy ways to reduce stress in order to help you study more effectively. Stress is a major cause of many serious health problems. Unfortunately, many people reduce stress by smoking, drinking alcohol, or eating too much. These do help us relax temporarily but cause other serious health problems. Try to find healthy ways to reduce your stress. Exercising reduces stress and helps you relax. Spending time with people who make you feel good is relaxing. Listening to music is relaxing, too. Finding healthy ways to relax will not only help you stay healthy, but will make your study time more effective as well.

Apply the Strategy

Work with a small group. Add to the list of healthy ways to reduce stress:

1. Taking a hot bath or shower.

2. Listening to music.

(continued on next page)

3. Seeing a movie.

4. Meditating.

5. Talking to a friend.

6. Taking a nap.

_____

_____

_____

_____

Now think about how you reduce your stress. The next time you want to relax, try one of the healthy ways on this list.

PUTTING IT ALL TOGETHER

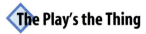

How healthy is your life and the way you live? Think about what you have learned in this chapter. Are there any changes you should make in your life? Are there any changes you want to make? Write about them in a short paragraph:

_____

_____

_____

_____

_____

_____

_____

_____

_____

_____

The Play's the Thing

Practice all the skills you have learned in this chapter. Practice and perform a short play. There are four scenes.

SCENE ONE

Actors: Two students. They are friends.

Situation: One student is sick. The other student gives advice about how to get better.

SCENE TWO

Actors: The sick student and a receptionist from the doctor's office.

Situation: The student who is sick calls the doctor's office to make an appointment.

SCENE THREE

Actors: The sick student and a doctor.

Situation: The student visits the doctor. The student describes his or her symptoms. The doctor gives the student advice on how to get well.

SCENE FOUR

Actors: The sick student and the friend from Scene One.

Situation: The friend asks the student how he or she is feeling. The student feels much better. They make plans to do something fun together.

1. There are five to eight roles. The sick student can be played by four different actors, one for each scene. Your teacher can assign roles, or you can choose a role. Every student should have a role in the play. Different groups of five to eight students can perform the play in different ways!

2. Work with the other actor in your scene. Practice the situation together.

3. Actors should perform the scenes.

Remember to applaud, or clap, for the actors!

 More Advice

There are many places to go for more advice on how to stay healthy. Here are a few for you to try.

1. Student Health Center. Health centers are there to help you, even when you are not sick. Go there and collect pamphlets or other handouts about staying healthy. Bring them to class to show your

classmates. Ask about free or low-cost health workshops and groups for preventing sickness and injury.

2. **Health Information Lines.** Call a health information line such as the one in this chapter. Report to your classmates on what you learned.

3. **The Internet.** The Internet has many web sites about health and fitness. Do a search for topics you are interested in. Or you can visit these useful sites. Report what you have learned to your classmates in a short presentation.

National Institutes of Health	www.nih.gov
National Cancer Institute	www.cancer.org
American Heart Association	www.amht.org
American Council on Science and Health	www.acsh.org
Web site on eating right	www.eatright.com
Web site for *Delicious* magazine	www.delicious-online.com

Test-Taking Tip

Go with your first guess on multiple choice questions. The first answer you choose is usually right. Don't change your answer unless you are sure that your first answer is wrong. If you do change your answer, make sure to erase your first answer completely before choosing a different answer.

CHECK YOUR PROGRESS

. . . .

On a scale of 1 to 5, rate how well you have mastered the goals set at the beginning of the chapter:

1 2 3 4 5 describe your symptoms.

1 2 3 4 5 understand and give advice.

1 2 3 4 5 know when to give strong advice and when to make suggestions.

1 2 3 4 5   practice telephone conversations before you call.

1 2 3 4 5   listen for sequence words and phrases.

1 2 3 4 5   pronounce /th/ correctly.

1 2 3 4 5   find healthy ways to reduce stress.

If you've given yourself a 3 or lower on any of these goals:

- visit the *Tapestry* web site for additional practice.
- ask your instructor for extra help.
- review the sections of the chapter that you found difficult.
- work with a partner or study group to further your progress.

These people all look different, but they are all Americans. With a partner, look at the photos carefully. Take turns with your partner describing each person. Share your descriptions with your classmates.

6

A HUMAN RAINBOW

What is the typical American or Canadian like? That is a difficult question, because the United States and Canada are made up of people who immigrated from many different countries. Even though the people of these two countries are many different colors, shapes, and sizes, they are all American or Canadian. All together, they make up a human rainbow.

Setting Goals

In this chapter you will:

- ◈ describe people and things.

- ◈ talk about similarities and differences in several different ways.

- ◈ learn to preview visuals in textbooks.

- ◈ find information from graphs.

- ◈ invent a title to summarize what you hear or read.

- ◈ pronounce the /er/ sound.

- ◈ use word games to practice English.

- ◈ use analogies to describe complex ideas.

- ◈ write about your family history.

◆**Getting Started**

Work with a partner. Do the following activities:

1. Look at the different photos and pictures of people in this chapter. What different kinds of people you see? Can you describe the people?

2. Find graphs and maps in this chapter. How many graphs are there? Look at the titles of the graphs. What kind of information do the graphs give?

3. In this chapter, you will play some word games. What word games do you already know? Do you play word games in your first language?

PART 1: Similarities

Although every person is different, there are many similarities among people of all cultures. This first section focuses on the way people are similar.

LANGUAGE YOU CAN USE: PHYSICAL DESCRIPTIONS

To describe people, use the verbs *to be* and *to have*. Study the following examples:

Kim is 20 years old.   Angela has curly hair.
Angela is average height.   Kim has brown eyes.

Kim is cute.   Angela has a beautiful smile.

Angela is thin.   Kim has small hands.

USING NEW LANGUAGE

Study the photos of the people on page 132. With your classmates, think of as many ways as you can to describe how the people look. Here are some words to help you. If you don't know the meaning of the words, ask your teacher for help.

Hair		Eyes	Features
long	brown	brown	freckles
short	blonde	blue	mustache
medium-length	red	green	beard
wavy	black	hazel	bangs
straight	brunette		mole
curly	light-brown		

Can you remember what people look like? In this exercise, you will practice describing your classmates. Your teacher will ask three students to go outside the classroom. After the students leave, the other students in the class will try to remember as many details as possible about the students outside the classroom. When the students come back in, compare the description with how they really look.

Do a similar activity. Work with a partner. Describe someone you know, such as a relative or friend whom your partner does not know. Ask your partner for details about the person he or she is describing.

Listening 1: Listen for Details

Look at the picture of Kim and Angela on page 134. Can you see any ways that they are similar? Listen to the tape. What other ways are Kim and Angela similar? Complete these statements.

1. They are both _____ years old.

2. Kim lives with _____, and Angela does too.

3. Kim's _____ is like Angela's _____.

4. They have the same number of _____ and _____.

5. Angela studies as _____ as Kim.

Discuss this with a partner. How are Kim and Angela similar?

LANGUAGE YOU CAN USE: TALKING ABOUT SIMILARITIES

In English there are several ways to say that people, things, or actions are similar. Read the following examples:

Kim and Angela are alike.   Kim is like Angela.

They are the same height.   Kim is as tall as Angela.

They have similar hair color.   Kim's hair is as dark as Angela's hair.

They are both happy.   Kim is happy, and Angela is too.

They like the same music.   Kim likes rock music, and so does Angela.

Notice that the sentence "They are the same height" and the sentence "Kim is as tall as Angela" have the same meaning. However, *height* is a noun and *tall* is an adjective. Study the examples again. Fill in the chart.

USING NEW LANGUAGE

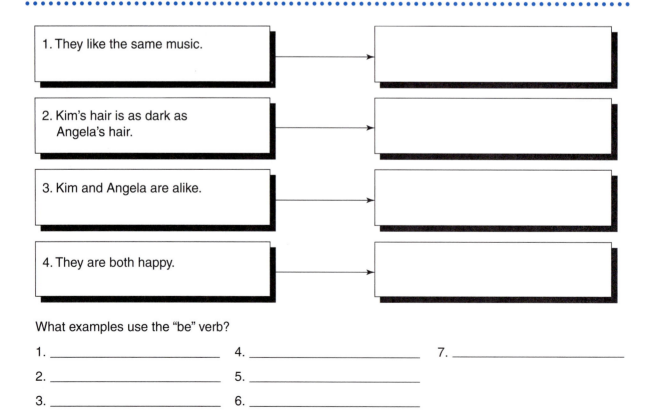

1. They like the same music.

2. Kim's hair is as dark as Angela's hair.

3. Kim and Angela are alike.

4. They are both happy.

What examples use the "be" verb?

1. _____   4. _____   7. _____

2. _____   5. _____

3. _____   6. _____

Which examples use the other verbs?

1. _____

2. _____

3. _____

Which examples use "as ___ as"?

1. _____

2. _____

Talk About It

Study the photos of these people carefully. Think about how they are similar. Work in a group of three students. The first group member tells one way the people in the photos are similar. Each of the other two group members must tell the same information in a different way. For example:

Ben, 22 years old, only child

Greg, 22 years old, only child

Student A: "They are the same age."

Student B: "They are both 22 years old."

Student C: "Ben is as old as Greg is."

Take turns being the first speaker.

More Practice

You can use the same forms to talk about things that are similar and places that are similar. For example, you can tell about similarities between two cities:

- Los Angeles is warm all year round, and Taipei is too.
- Los Angeles and Taipei are both crowded cities.
- Los Angeles has traffic problems, and so does Taipei.

Think about two cities that are similar. Work with a partner. Tell your partner three things that are similar between the two cities you are thinking of.

PART 2: Rainbow of Diversity

Now that you can describe similarities, let's look at ways to describe differences.

ACADEMIC POWER STRATEGY

Preview visuals in textbooks to help you prepare for classes. Many textbooks contain pictures, photos, graphs, maps, and other visual information. Studying the visual information in a textbook can help you prepare for class. Pictures and photos illustrate important information. Graphs summarize and give a visual picture of complex information. Studying the visual material in your book is a good way to get ready to listen to your professor or to prepare to read a textbook. Before you go to class, look at the graphs and pictures in the chapter you will be discussing. This will help you understand what you hear in class. It will also help you prepare for class discussions.

Apply the Strategy

This exercise uses a "pie graph" (sometimes called a "circle graph"). Work with a partner. Study this graph. Then answer the questions.

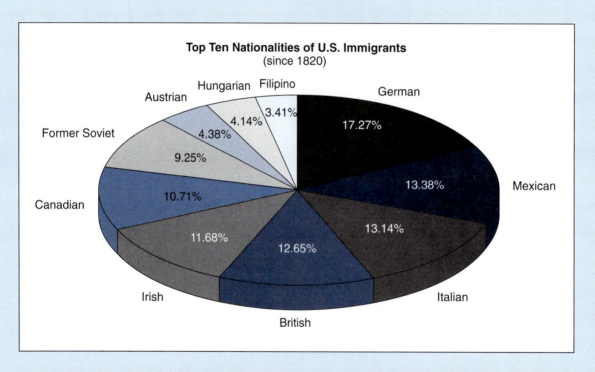

Top Ten Nationalities of U.S. Immigrants
(since 1820)

- Hungarian
- Filipino 3.41%
- Austrian 4.14%
- German 17.27%
- Former Soviet 4.38%
- 9.25%
- Mexican 13.38%
- Canadian 10.71%
- Italian 13.14%
- Irish 11.68%
- British 12.65%

1. What percentage of the population is each ethnic group?

2. Which ethnic group has the largest population?

3. Which group has the smallest population?

◀Talking About Graphs

This kind of graph is called a "bar graph." Before you discuss this graph, study it carefully. Think about what kind of information it shows.

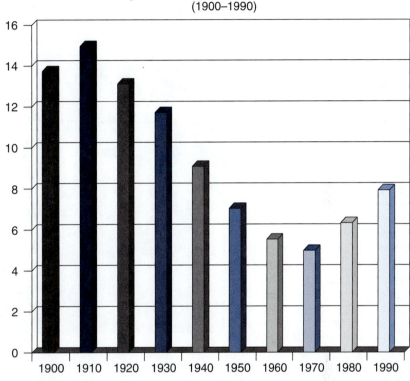

Percentage of U.S. Population that was Foreign-born
(1900–1990)

Look at the graph with your partner. Use the information from the graph to talk about the answers to these questions:

1. What do you think "foreign-born" means?

2. What year was the largest percentage of the U.S. population foreign-born?

3. What year was the smallest percentage of the U.S. population foreign-born?

4. Does it look like the recent percentage of foreign-born citizens is increasing, decreasing, or staying about the same?

5. Why do you think the graph only shows data for every 10 years?

◆**Practice Reading Graphs**   Today, many newspapers, magazines, and books use graphs to explain complex information. Find a graph in a newspaper, magazine, or book. Share your graph with your classmates. Explain what the graph means.

◆**Getting Ready to Listen**   Study these maps and the photo before you listen. Work with a partner to try to guess what the speaker will talk about.

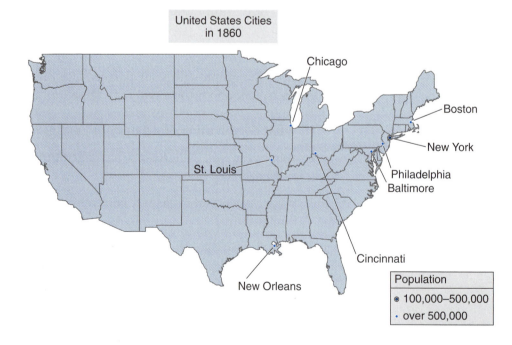

United States Cities in 1900

St. Paul
Minneapolis
Milwaukee
Chicago
Rochester
Buffalo
Syracuse
Worcester
Boston
Providence
New Haven
New York
Scranton
Philadelphia
Baltimore
Washington, D.C.
Pittsburgh
Cleveland
Columbus
Cincinnati
Louisville
Detroit
Denver
Omaha
Toledo
Kansas City
St. Louis
San Francisco
Los Angeles
Memphis
Indianapolis
New Orleans

Population
⊚ 100,000–500,000
· over 500,000

 Listen

Listening 2: Immigration

Listen to this passage carefully. Complete these three main ideas. Listen to the passage again to check your answers.

1. Before 1860, most people: _____

2. Cities grew bigger because: _____

3. Immigrants lived: _____

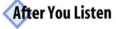 **After You Listen**

Study the maps and photo again. How did they help you understand the listening passage?

LANGUAGE LEARNING STRATEGY

Invent a title to summarize what you hear or read. A title is a short statement that explains the main idea. One way to check to see if you understand the main idea of a passage is to invent a title for that passage. When you listen to people talk or read something without a title, try to invent a title that summarizes the main idea.

(continued on next page)

Apply the Strategy

Work with a partner. Listen to each of these stories about different kinds of Americans and Canadians. With your partner, discuss what you think is the main idea of each passage. Invent a title for each passage.

1. Title: _____

2. Title: _____

Culture Note

When Columbus arrived in the Americas, he thought he was in India, so he called the people "Indians." Today we call these people "Native Americans."

3. Title: _____

4. Title: _____

There are many people in the United States today whose ancestors came from Africa as slaves. These people are usually called African Americans. African Americans prefer this name rather than "Blacks." African Americans were once called "Negroes" or "colored people." These names are considered offensive today.

LANGUAGE YOU CAN USE: TALKING ABOUT DIFFERENCES

In English, there are several ways to say that people, things, or places are different. Read these examples:

- Rachel and Michael are different.
- There are differences between Jean-Marc and Billy.
- There are more African Americans than Native Americans in the United States.
- Jean-Marc is taller than Rachel is.
- There are fewer Hispanics than African Americans.
- Billy isn't as old as Michael is.
- Michael and Billy differ in height.

There are three comparatives in English that have irregular forms: *good, bad,* and *far.* Look at these examples:

1. good > better

The cake is good. The ice cream is better than the cake.

2. bad > worse

My car is in bad shape, but his car is in worse shape than mine is.

3. far > farther

It is far to Atlanta, but Seattle is even farther.

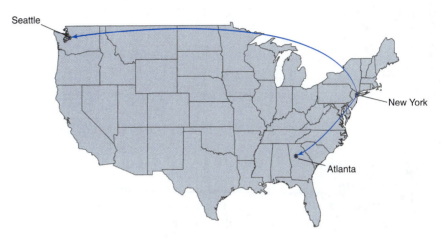

USING NEW LANGUAGE

Your teacher will choose a partner for you. Then follow these instructions:

1. Don't speak to your partner at first. Just look at him or her.

2. Make some notes on how you are similar to and different from your partner. Consider physical features like height, hair color, and eye color. Also consider other things, like your personalities and activities you like to do.

3. With your partner, make a list of at least five ways that you are similar and five ways that you are different.

4. Share your list with your classmates.

5. Ask your classmates if they can find any more similarities or differences between you and your partner.

Talk About It

You can also talk about how places and things are different. What is a typical food from your native country? Work with a group of students. Describe a food from your native country. Tell how the food is different from other foods. Use the chart on the following page to take notes on the different foods described by your classmates. Ask your group members questions about the foods they describe so you can be sure you understand what the food is like.

Your teacher will give you a partner from another group. Tell your partner about the food from your native country. Then tell your partner what you learned about other foods.

NAME	COUNTRY	NAME OF FOOD	DESCRIPTION

Which of the foods that you learned about would you like to try?

The Sound of It: Pronouncing the /er/ Sound

One of the most difficult sounds to pronounce in English is the /er/ sound like at the end of *better.* Listen to native speakers of English and pay attention to how they pronounce the /er/ sound. Read the following sentences aloud. Pay special attention to the /er/ sound.

1. I am taller than my sister is.

2. She is smarter than I am when it comes to math.

3. She is better at algebra than I am.

4. She makes fewer mistakes than I do.

More Practice

There are many words that end in *er* in English. Work with a partner. Make phrases with adjectives and nouns that end in *er*. Write the words in a table like the one below. The first one has been done for you as an example. Exchange your list with another group. Practice saying the phrases from the other group's list.

1. better   partner
2.
3.
4.
5.
6.
7.
8.
9.
10.

PART 3: The Salad Bowl

> The United States is a society of immigrants, each of whom began life anew, on an equal footing. This is the secret of America—a nation of people with the fresh memory of old traditions who dare to explore new frontiers.
>
> —JOHN F. KENNEDY

In this section you will learn how immigrants have made their marks on the culture of the United States and Canada.

TUNING IN

This video explains the problems that some immigrants have when they first come to the United States. Read the questions below. Watch the video, looking for the answers to the questions. Write the answers to the questions. Watch the video again to check your answers. After you finish, invent a title for this video that reflects the main idea. Compare your title with your classmates' titles. Choose the best title.

© CNN

1. What problem do these immigrants have?

2. Where are they from?

3. How are they solving their problem?

4. What changes do they need to make in order to be successful in the United States?

A good title for this video is _____.

Talking About Immigrant Problems

What are some other problems that people have when they immigrate to another country? Here is a list of problems that immigrants may have when they go to another country. Are there any other problems that immigrants have? With your classmates, complete this chart by thinking of other problems. Then think of some things immigrants can do to solve these problems.

Problem	Solution
1. different customs in the new country	• learn as much as possible about the customs • ask questions about customs • make friends
2. different language in the new country	
3. different foods	
4. different kinds of stores	
5.	
6.	

◀ **Getting Ready to Read**   The following reading selection uses an **analogy** to make a complex idea clearer. Usually, an analogy explains how a real object is similar to a complex idea. For example, you might say that learning a new language is like a baby learning to walk.

  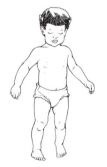 

The baby starts out crawling.　　**Then she begins to stand by herself.**　　**When she feels comfortable, she tries to take a few steps.**　　**In the end she is walking and even running.**

Learning a new language is similar because at first it is slow and difficult. Eventually, you try to say some things by yourself, and in the end you are talking like a native speaker. Can you think of another analogy for learning a new language?

Look for the analogy in this reading. How does the analogy make the idea more clear?

Immigrants to the United States have had a big influence on the food Americans eat. Two of the most typical American foods, the frankfurter (or hot dog) and pizza, actually come from Germany and Italy.

Read

The Statue of Liberty in New York Harbor was one of the first things that European immigrants saw when they came to the United States. It has been called the symbol of hope and freedom for the poor immigrants who came to the United States between 1886 and 1915.

The "Salad Bowl"

1 Many people immigrate to the United States and Canada. The first immigrants to the United States were from England and the Netherlands. The first immigrants to Canada were from France and England. When they arrived in the new land, there were already people here—the Native Americans or Indians.

2 Over hundreds of years, more people came. They came from Europe, Latin America, Asia, Africa, and Australia. Immigrants from many different countries and nationalities have mixed together to become Canadians and Americans. Even though they are now Canadians and Americans, immigrants keep some of the foods, customs, and holiday celebrations from their native cultures. The groups of people mix together like vegetables in a giant salad. That is why the United States and Canada are sometimes called a "Salad Bowl."

3 In a salad, each vegetable—lettuce, tomato, and carrot—keeps its own flavor, but they all taste better when they are mixed together. It is the same way with the people in Canada and the United States. Each group of people keeps its own flavor, but the people become better when they mix with other immigrants. They are more creative and open-minded when they interact with people from other groups.

4 Most Canadians and Americans like the diversity and new ideas that immigrants bring. After all, except for the Native Americans, they are all immigrants too. However, not all people welcome the immigrants. These people are afraid that the immigrants will change their culture or take their jobs. Today, the United States and Canada both limit the number of immigrants who come to their countries.

5   What do you think? Should countries like the United States and Canada limit immigration? What are the advantages and disadvantages of being a nation of immigrants?

◆After You Read

Vocabulary Building

Answer the clues to complete this puzzle. All of the words in the puzzle are found in the reading passage.

1. A country in North America.

2. A person who goes to another country to live.

3. The way something tastes is its _____.

4. A party.

5. To mix and talk with other people.

6. A _____ is made of lettuce, tomatoes, and other vegetables.

7. Someone who will listen to new ideas is _____.

8. Someone who builds, designs, or makes new things is

   _____.

9. A day with no school or work.

1. ___ ___ ___ ___ D ___

      2. I ___ ___ ___ ___ ___ ___ ___ ___

3. ___ ___ ___ V ___ ___

4. ___ ___ ___ E ___ ___ ___ ___ ___ ___

5. ___ ___ ___ ___ R ___ ___ ___

      6. S ___ ___ ___ ___

7. ___ ___ ___ ___ ___ I ___ ___ ___ ___

8. ___ ___ ___ ___ T ___ ___ ___

9. ___ ___ ___ ___ ___ ___ Y

1. Canada, 2. Immigrant, 3. Flavor, 4. Celebration, 5. Interact, 6. Salad, 7. Open-minded, 8. Creative, 9. Holiday

LANGUAGE LEARNING STRATEGY

Use word games to practice English. Do you have a favorite word game? English speakers like to do word puzzles and play word games. Word games are a good way to practice the language.

Apply the Strategy

Look at the word games in this chapter. Do you know any other word games? Find a word game in a magazine or newspaper. Bring it to class and work with your classmates to complete it.

 Try It Out

Analogies are one way to make a comparison between two things. Another way to make comparisons is with **similes.** Similes use the word *like* or *as* to compare two things. For example:

My little sister is like a fly. She buzzes around just to annoy me.

Now my backpack is as light as a feather. I took all of the books out of it.

1. Men are like . . .

2. Women are as . . .

3. Studying English is like . . .

4. Using a computer is as . . .

5. Getting an *A* on a test is like . . .

6. Going shopping is as . . .

> Some word games, like riddles, have a very old tradition. The ancient Egyptians had riddles. Other word games, like crossword puzzles, are more recent inventions. The first crossword puzzle was published in 1913 and was called a "word-cross." About thirty million people in the United States spend a part of every day doing a crossword puzzle.

Think of two more beginnings of sentences. Exchange your sentence beginnings with another student and complete each other's sentences.

Word Game—Think Fast

Think Fast is another kind of word game. Before you play this game, make sure you read the procedures and rules of the game. If you are not sure you understand the rules, ask your teacher to demonstrate for you.

Procedures

1. Divide your class evenly into teams with four people on each team.

2. Your teacher will give one team member a list of words.

3. He or she will read the category at the top of the list to his or her group members.

4. He or she will try to get the other team members to guess the words on the list by giving them clues.

5. The team has 1 minute to guess as many words as possible. Do not spend too much time on one word. If the team gets stuck, go on to the next word and come back to that word later.

6. The team that guesses the most words wins.

Rules

1. The person giving the clues can say a sentence or the beginning of a sentence as a clue. For example, if the word is *baker,* he or she can say, "This is a person." "This person works with food." "She's not a chef; she's a _____."

2. The person giving clues cannot use his or her hands (sit on your hands if this is difficult for you).

3. The person giving the clues cannot say a word that is almost the same as the word the team is trying to guess. For example, if the word is *baker,* he or she cannot say *bake, baking, bakery,* or any other word that has *bake* in it.

4. The person giving the clues can use English words only.

After you play, think about the game you just played. Which clues worked the best? If you don't know the exact word for something in English, what questions can you use to find out the word from a native speaker of English?

One group of immigrants that has influenced the United States is the Irish. The Irish holiday of St. Patrick's Day is celebrated on March 17 in the United States. Most people recognize St. Patrick's Day by wearing something green, even if they are not Irish.

What do you know about your ancestors? Did they speak the same languages that you do? What kind of jobs did they have in the past? What do you know about where they have lived? Have they ever immigrated? If they have, why did they immigrate?

Tell a partner everything you know about your ancestors. Listen to your partner's description of his or her ancestors. Ask your partner questions about things that are unclear. If you are unsure of some answers, ask your parents or grandparents about your ancestors. Write a short paragraph about the history of your family.

PUTTING IT ALL TOGETHER

Your teacher may assign one or all of the activities below:

 Role Play

Role plays are a kind of unplanned play or drama where the people act like they think someone else might in a certain situation. Role plays are a good way to practice English because you can pretend that you are someone else.

Work with a partner. Choose one of the role plays below, or your teacher may assign you a role play. Practice the role play with a partner. Perform your role play for the rest of the class.

1. You came to a party with a friend. The party is very crowded. You are ready to go home, but you cannot find your friend anywhere. Talk to someone you have met at the party. Describe your friend and ask if he or she has seen your friend.

2. Your boyfriend or girlfriend lives in another city. A friend asks you about him or her. Describe your boyfriend or girlfriend to your friend.

3. You see a small child at the playground. The child doesn't seem to have any adults around. Describe the child to a police officer.

4. Your teacher asks you "Who was your teacher last semester?" You cannot remember your teacher's name. Describe your old teacher to your new teacher.

5. Describe your sister or brother to someone who is looking for a date.

6. You just saw a car accident. The person who caused the accident drove away, but you got a good look at the person. Describe the person who caused the accident to the police.

7. Your grandmother is visiting you from another city. She went out for a walk in the park and hasn't returned yet. You are getting a little worried. Ask a man in the park if he has seen your grandmother.

8. You went to a movie last night. One of the actors in the movie is very familiar to you, but you can't remember his name. Describe the actor to your friend and ask him or her to help you remember his name.

9. You bought a coffee maker, but when you took it home and tried to use it, it didn't work. When you take the coffee maker back to the store, the salesperson asks you to describe the clerk who sold it to you.

10. You can't get away from your job to pick up your mother at the airport. Your friend has offered to pick up your mother, but your friend doesn't know what your mother looks like. Describe your mother to your friend.

Information Gap

Look at this graph while your partner looks at the graph on the next page. Each graph is missing some information. Ask your partner questions to complete the graph. Write the missing information on your graph. Answer the questions your partner asks you.

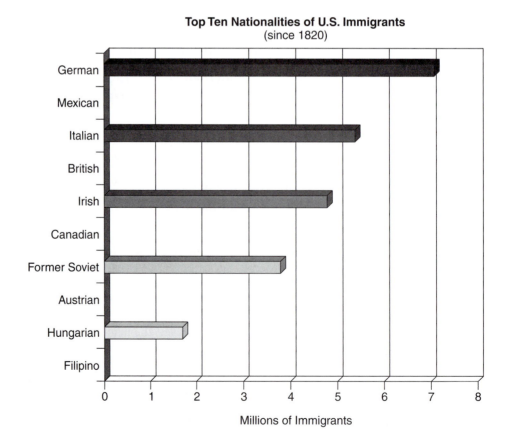

Top Ten Nationalities of U.S. Immigrants
(since 1820)

Millions of Immigrants

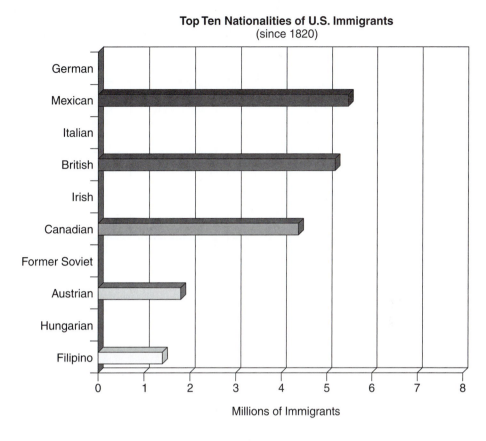

Top Ten Nationalities of U.S. Immigrants
(since 1820)

Millions of Immigrants

Tongue Twister

One way to practice difficult sounds is by saying tongue twisters. Practice this tongue twister. It will help you pronounce the /er/ sound.

> Once upon a barren moor,
> There was a bear, also a boar.
> The bear could not bear the boar.
> The boar thought the bear a bore.
> At last the bear could bear no more
> Of that boar that bored him on the moor,
> And so one morn he bored the boar—
> That boar will bore the bear no more.

Four Across

Here is another word game called Four Across. Read the procedures and rules carefully, and then play the game.

Procedures

1. Work with a partner.

2. Make a chart on a piece of paper. Make the boxes big enough so that you can write several words in each box. See the example chart on page 156.

3. Your teacher will choose four different letters of the alphabet. Write each letter in the boxes in the left column.

	Outside Activities	Colors	Animals	Drinks

Rules

1. When your teacher says "Go," you and your partner have five minutes to think of as many words as possible for each category that begin with the letters of the alphabet your teacher chose. For example, if the category is "food" and the letter is "s," you might write steak, sausage, sauce, strawberry, etc.

2. When the teacher says "Stop," you must stop writing.

3. Compare your answers with another pair's answers. For each answer that is the same, the pair gets one point. For each answer that is different, the pair gets two points.

Test-Taking Tip

If you know you will be absent on the day a test will be given, talk to your instructor as soon as possible. Explain why you won't be able to come to class that day. Let your instructor know that you want to arrange a make-up test. Be prepared to take a make-up test earlier than the date of the official test.

CHECK YOUR PROGRESS

On a scale of 1 to 5, rate how well you have mastered the goals set at the beginning of the chapter:

1 2 3 4 5   describe people and things.

1 2 3 4 5   talk about similarities and differences in several different ways.

1 2 3 4 5   learn to preview visuals in textbooks.

1 2 3 4 5   find information from graphs.

1 2 3 4 5   invent a title to summarize what you hear or read.

1 2 3 4 5   pronounce the /er/ sound.

1 2 3 4 5   use word games to practice English.

1 2 3 4 5   understand analogies that describe complex ideas.

1 2 3 4 5   write about your family history.

If you've given yourself a 3 or lower on any of these goals:

- visit the *Tapestry* web site for additional practice.
- ask your instructor for extra help.
- review the sections of the chapter that you found difficult.
- work with a partner or study group to further your progress.

L ook at the photos. These people are all heroes. They have all won the Nobel Peace Prize. Who are they? What did they do? Discuss these questions with your classmates.

MY HERO

Heroes are people whom we admire. They are people who live well and do great things. Who is a person you admire? Do you know someone who lives well or does exceptional things? In this chapter, you will hear about some famous Canadian and American heroes. You will also learn about a fictional superhero. Finally, you will talk about your personal heroes. You will describe the people who have made a difference in your life.

Setting Goals

In this chapter you will learn how to:

◈ use a chart to help you take good notes when you listen.

◈ describe people's personalities.

◈ use adjectives to make descriptions.

◈ pronounce the long *e* sound correctly.

◈ elaborate on your answers.

◈ use music to help you learn English and improve your pronunciation.

◈ find a mentor.

Some words in English change over time. For example, *heroine* has been used as a word to describe a female hero. Now most English speakers use *hero* to describe both men and women.

Getting Started

1. Look at the photos and pictures of people in this chapter. Many of these people are famous. How many of these people do you recognize?

2. Some of the pictures are of people who are not real. People who are not real are called "fictional." Look through the photos and pictures again. Work with a partner. Identify which people in this chapter are fictional and which are real people.

PART 1: Twentieth Century Heroes

In this section, you will learn about twentieth-century heroes. Some heroes you know already. Other heroes might be new to you.

In the United States, a "hero sandwich" is a big sandwich made with cheese, cold cuts, and a loaf of French bread. It is also sometimes called a submarine sandwich. How do you think this sandwich got its name?

Getting Ready to Listen

Look at the next page. Do you know these heroes? Some of them are heroes because of their athletic abilities or talents. Some are heroes because of their intelligence or the work they do to help sick or poor people. Some are heroes because they are role models—they are successful even though their life has been difficult.

Work with a partner. Tell your partner which heroes you know. Tell your partner what you know about each of these heroes. If you do not know anything about these heroes, look at the pictures and guess what they do.

A. Hillary Clinton

B. Bob Marley

E. Florence Griffith Joyner

Martin Luther King, Jr., won the Nobel Peace Prize in 1964. Mother Teresa of Calcutta won the prize in 1979, and Rigoberta Menchu was the winner in 1992.

C. Celine Dion

D. Sammy Sosa

Listen

Listening 1: Heroes

You will hear descriptions of these heroes. Match the heroes with their descriptions.

Description 1 _____

Description 2 _____

Description 3 _____

Description 4 _____

Description 5 _____

◆ **After You Listen**   Of these people, who do you think is the biggest hero? Why?

LANGUAGE LEARNING STRATEGY

U se a chart to help you take good notes when you listen. Using a chart is one way to organize your notes. Using a chart can help you focus on what you are listening to. A chart helps you compare information about similar things. It helps you understand now and remember what you heard later.

Apply the Strategy

Listen to the stories of the heroes again. Use this chart to take notes as you listen. Listen for the information in the chart. The first one has been done for you as an example.

Name	Where is he/she from?	Athlete? Entertainer? Political Person?	Two acomplishments	Living?
Flo Jo	America (Los Angeles)	Athlete	1. won Olympic gold medal 2. 1988 sports woman of the year	No

LANGUAGE YOU CAN USE: DESCRIBING PEOPLE

Adjectives are words that describe people, places, or things. You can use adjectives with a *be* verb or before a noun in a sentence:

Subject + *be* + adjective *or* Subject + *be* + adjective + noun.

> Michael Jordan *is tall*. He *was* a *fantastic* basketball player. Michael *is* very *athletic*. He *was* the *best* player on the Chicago Bulls.

In English, adjectives do not change for plural nouns. Study these examples:

> Martin Luther King and Mother Teresa were *powerful* leaders.

> Celine Dion and Wayne Greztky are *Canadian* celebrities.

Not:

> Martin Luther King and Mother Teresa were ~~*powerfuls*~~ leaders.

> Celine Dion and Wayne Gretzky are ~~*Canadians*~~ heroes.

Here are some useful adjectives to describe heroes. Put a check mark next to the ones you know. Use a dictionary to learn the words you don't know.

_____ kind	_____ hardworking
_____ peaceful	_____ talented
_____ caring	_____ dedicated
_____ helpful	_____ Canadian
_____ strong	_____ heroic
_____ intelligent	_____ American
_____ amazing	_____ funny
_____ creative	_____ athletic
_____ brave	_____ feminine
_____ powerful	

USING NEW LANGUAGE

Work with a partner. Describe the heroes pictured on page 164. Use these adjectives to make complete sentences about the heroes. Use the two different forms for each photo. For example:

Mother Teresa was a caring person.

She was kind to poor people.

**Rigaberta Menchu
(brave, peaceful)**

**Hillary Rodham Clinton
(intelligent, American)**

Mother Theresa (kind, caring)

Bob Marley (creative, talented)

**Martin Luther King, Jr.
(peaceful, intelligent)**

**Celine Dion
(talented, caring)**

Sammy Sosa (helpful, strong)

**Florence Griffith Joyner
(dedicated, feminine)**

 **Brainstorming**

What other adjectives can be used to describe heroes? With your classmates, brainstorm a list of as many words as you can think of. Your teacher will write the list of words on the chalkboard.

 **Small Group Discussion**

Do you know of any other heroes that might fit into each category? How many additional heroes can you think of? Use adjectives to describe them.

PART 2: Superhero

Superheroes usually have super powers. They can do things that normal humans cannot do. This section tells about superheroes.

 Getting Ready to Listen

Who are the people in this picture? Have you ever seen them before? What do you know about them? With your classmates, make a list of all the things that you know about these fictional people.

 Listen

Listening 2: Superman

Listen to the tape about Superman to understand the main idea. Then listen to the tape again for details. Finish the lists based on the information from the tape.

SUPERMAN	HE WEARS	HE CAN
1. tall	1. blue tights	1. _____
2. _____	2. red _____	2. _____
3. broad _____	3. big _____	3. bend a steel rod
4. dark _____		

CLARK KENT	CLARK WEARS	LOIS LANE
1. Superman	1. not blue tights	1. _____
2. _____	2. _____	2. _____
3. _____	3. _____	3. good reporter

◀ After You Listen

What did you learn about Superman? Have you heard of any of these other fictional heroes?

Hercules   Spiderman   Paul Bunyan   Batman   Sherlock Holmes

Who are some other fictional heroes that you know? With your class, make a list of fictional heroes.

◀ Getting Ready to Read

What do you think these two men have to do with Superman? Work with a partner to think of how they might be connected.

◀ Read

Jerry Siegal and Joe Shuster, the creators of Superman.

The Real Story of Superman

1   Superman is the original superhero. Two young boys from Ohio, Jerry Siegal and Joe Shuster, created Superman as a comic strip when they were in high school. Joe was the artist. He made the pictures. Jerry wrote the stories. In 1938, they sold their comics for $10 per page.

2   The Superman story made millions of dollars. Superman has been the hero of a radio show, several cartoons, TV shows, and movies. He's also in books and video games. Yet Jerry and Joe didn't **get rich** from Superman. They sold Superman to Detective Comics in 1938 for a salary of $15 per week! But this **story has a happy ending.** In 1975, many of the **newspapers that carried Superman comics** agreed to pay Joe and Jerry for their creative idea.

3   Of course, the Superman story is fiction. There are some things about it that are difficult to believe. One of these is the fact that no one recognizes that Clark Kent is really Superman. **He fools everyone** with those thick glasses. It is also **a little funny**

that he represents the best qualities of an American hero. Super-man always fights for truth, justice, and the American way. Yet he's not an American at all. He's not even human. He's an alien from the planet Krypton.

4   Even though the Superman story has some parts that are difficult to believe, it's still one of the greatest hero stories ever. In 1998, *Entertainment Weekly* chose the Superman story among the top ten of science-fiction stories ever. Joe and Jerry, those two creative teenagers, will never be forgotten.

◆ Vocabulary Building

Sometimes it is easier to remember small groups of words (phrases) than individual words. Look at these phrases. Go back to the story and find them. Choose the best definition for each phrase based on the context in the reading.

1. get rich

    a. get a job   b. make money

2. story has a happy ending

    a. everything turns out well   b. everyone is laughing at the end

3. newspapers carried Superman comics

    a. Superman comics were in the newspaper
    b. Superman comics were important to newspapers

4. he fools everyone

    a. he jokes with everyone   b. he keeps the truth from everyone

5. a little funny

    a. strange   b. laughing

TUNING IN: "Super Barrio!"

This video tells about a hero from Mexico. He tries to help the poor people in Mexico. He calls himself Super Barrio! But he is not a typical superhero. With your classmates, finish this list of characteristics of a typical superhero. Watch the video. Then explain why Super Barrio is not a typical superhero.

Typical Superhero

1. a man or woman with strong muscles

2. _____

3. _____

4. _____

© CNN

◆ **Guess the Meaning**

Before you watch the video, read this list of words and phrases. Circle the definition that goes with each word or phrase. Watch the video. Check to see if your answers are correct.

1. Caped Crusader

   a. a superhero

   b. a religious hero

2. doesn't ripple with muscle

   a. isn't in shape

   b. doesn't work hard

3. a man of the people

   a. a friendly man

   b. a man who helps poor people

4. high school dropout

   a. well educated

   b. didn't finish high school

5. bottom rung of society

   a. short people

   b. poor people

6. unveil a statue

   a. make a statue

   b. present a statue

◆ **Think About It**

Compare Super Barrio to Superman. How are they similar? How are they different? Is Super Barrio a real hero or a fictional hero? Watch the video again. Discuss this question with your classmates.

◆ **The Sound of It: The Long e Sound**

In the 1950s, the *Superman* TV show began this way: "Faster than a speeding bullet! More powerful than a locomotive! Able to leap tall buildings in a single bound! Look up in the sky! It's a bird! It's a plane! No, it's Superman!"

Can you say this as though you were the announcer of the TV show?

One of the most difficult sounds to say in English is the long *e* sound as in the words *speeding* and *leap*. Listen to your teacher say the following pairs of words. Can you hear the difference between them?

1. leap   lip
2. seat   sit
3. meat   mitt
4. green   grin
5. feet   fit
6. heat   hit
7. leave   live
8. peak   pick
9. sleep   slip
10. eat   it
11. lead   lid
12. deep   dip

> **It is easier to say the words with a long _e_ sound if you make a tight smile with your mouth. That's why North Americans say "cheese" when they take a photo.**

◆ Practice New Sounds

Now work with a partner. Practice saying these sentences. Listen to your partner, and make sure that he or she pronounces the long _e_ sound correctly. If possible, record yourself saying the words on the list. Listen to the tape. Do you pronounce the words correctly?

You must heat the
meat before you eat it.

My feet fit into
these shoes.

I couldn't stop! There was
a deep dip in the road.

Sit in the seat, but
don't fall asleep.

Now say this again:

"Faster than a speeding bullet! More powerful than a locomotive!
Able to leap tall buildings in a single bound! Look up in the sky! It's
a bird! It's a plane! No, it's Superman!"

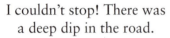 **Small Group Activity**

Sometimes it is easier to practice speaking another language when
you pretend to be someone different. This speaking exercise allows
you to pretend you are someone else.

Work together with a group of students. Look at the cartoon
strip on the next page. Then follow these steps:

1. With your group members, invent dialogue for the characters to say.

2. Each member of the group should take the role of one of the
   characters in the cartoon script.

3. Continue the story by saying what you think the characters
   would do next.

4. Perform your dialogue for your other classmates. Videotape or
   audiotape your dialogues so that you can hear and see what you
   sound like in English.

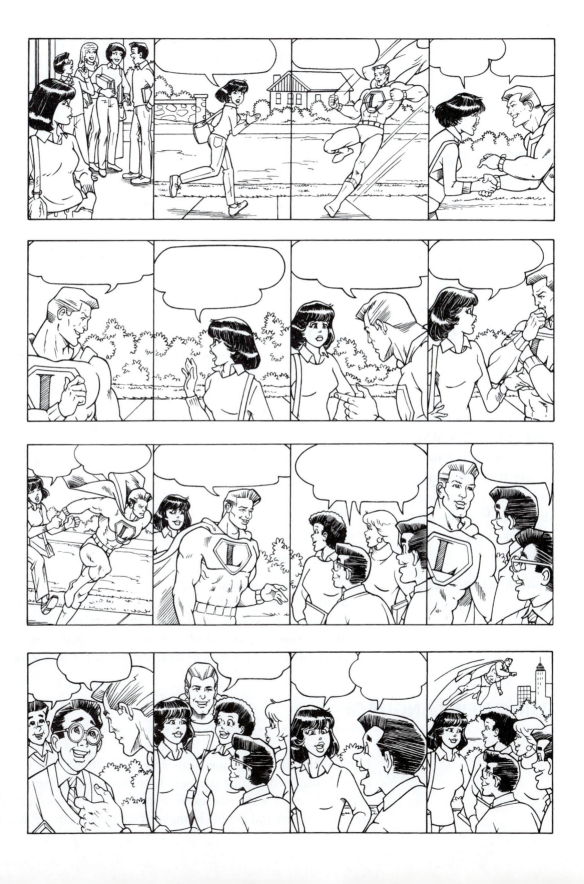

After you perform your dialogue for your classmates, watch or listen to the tape of the dialogue. What do you like about the dialogue? What would make it better? You can do this activity with your favorite cartoon strip. Just take out the words and make up your own.

PART 3: Personal Heroes

Most people have a personal hero or heroes. A personal hero is someone you admire. A personal hero can be anyone you look up to. A personal hero can be someone you know, a famous living person, or a person who lived a long time ago. The hero can be real or fictional.

LANGUAGE YOU CAN USE: ELABORATING ON ANSWERS

> I have a dream that my four little children will one day live in a nation where they will not be judged by the color of their skin, but by the content of their character.
>
> —MARTIN LUTHER KING, JR.

Answering questions is important in class, at work, and in daily life. Sometimes a short answer is fine. However, you can make a more interesting answer if you give reasons, information, and details. This is called **elaborating** on an answer. Elaborating helps the listener understand the reasons for your answer. Look at these examples:

Short answer:

Q: Who is your personal hero?
A: Martin Luther King, Jr.

Elaborated answer:

Q: Who is your personal hero?
A: Martin Luther King, Jr., is my hero because he was a strong leader. He stood up for what he believed in. He tried to change people's ideas about prejudice and racism. He changed people's ideas in peaceful ways. He was a great teacher, speaker, and leader.

USING NEW LANGUAGE

Look at the following questions and think about how you will answer them. Work with a partner. Take turns asking these questions. When you answer the questions, explain your reasons, and give extra information and details to make your answers more interesting.

1. Who was your hero when you were a child?

2. Who was your hero when you were in high school?

3. Who is your hero now?

4. Who are the heroes in your native country?

5. Who is the hero you would most like to meet someday?

 **Getting Ready to Listen**

Listen to these people talk about their personal heroes. Before you listen, think about your personal hero or heroes. Tell a partner the name of your hero(es).

 Listen

Listening 3: Personal Heroes

Listen to the tape. Try to understand the main ideas that Kate, Robert, and Nancy are talking about. Then listen to the tape again. Here are some of the things said about these heroes. Write what each hero did under his or her name. The first one has been done for you as an example.

- helped poor people

- soldiers

- won the Nobel Peace Prize

- against racism

- helped sick people

- are well-known by Native American people

- was peaceful

Dr. Martin Luther King	Mother Teresa of Calcutta	Navajo Code-Talkers
_____	_helped poor people_	_____
_____	_____	_____

◆**After You Listen**   What new information did you learn about the heroes from this exercise? Talk about what you learned with a partner.

LANGUAGE LEARNING STRATEGY

Use music to help you learn English and improve your pronunciation. Singing songs can help you improve your English. You can remember new words and phrases more easily if you hear them in a song. Most songs repeat words so the words are easier to remember. Music and songs also help you with the rhythm and pronunciation of English. Most songs have rhyming words that help practice pronunciation.

Apply the Strategy   Dr. Martin Luther King, Jr. was Robert's hero in the previous exercise. Dr. King tried to eliminate discrimination against races in the United States. "We Will Overcome" was a theme song for people who fought for equality. It is a song of hope for a time when there will be no more racism. It is not a difficult song. Listen to the song. Read the words as you listen. When you feel comfortable, sing along with the tape.

We Will Overcome
....

1.   We will overcome. We will overcome. We will overcome someday.

    Oh, deep in my heart. I do believe; we will overcome someday.

2.   We are not afraid. We are not afraid. We are not afraid today.
   Oh, deep in my heart. I do believe; we are not afraid today.
3.   We'll walk hand in hand. We'll walk hand in hand. We'll walk hand in hand someday.
   Oh, deep in my heart. I do believe; we'll walk hand in hand someday.
4.   We will live in peace. We will live in peace. We will live in peace someday.
   Oh, deep in my heart. I do believe; we will live in peace someday.
5.   We will overcome. We will overcome. We will overcome someday.
   Oh, deep in my heart I do believe; we will overcome someday.

The song "We Will Overcome" has some words with the long *e* sound—for example, *we, deep, believe,* and *peace.* Sing the song again. Pay attention to how you sing the long *e* sound.

◆ A Song About a Hero

"We Will Overcome" was originally a religious song. The words have been changed to fit many different occasions. These words were used by African Americans to protest against racism. Mexican Americans translated the song into Spanish when they protested against unfair labor policies.

There are several other songs in English about heroes. "John Henry" is a song about a fictional African American hero. In the song, John Henry is a man who works making a railroad tunnel through a mountain. He works with a hammer and piece of steel to cut the rock. In the song, John Henry challenges a steam-powered machine that drills a hole in the mountain. He tries to cut the rock faster than the steam-powered drill. In the song, John Henry wins the race, but he works so hard that he dies.

This song is a little more difficult than "We Will Overcome." Follow these steps to learn the song:

1. Read the words to the song aloud together with your classmates.

2. Pay attention to the pronunciation, rhythm, and rhyme of the song.

3. Circle the rhyming words.

4. Go through the song line by line with your teacher. Make sure you know the meaning of the words in the song.

5. Listen to the song as you read the words.

6. Listen to the song again. Sing the song when you feel comfortable.

John Henry
· · · · · · · · · · · ·

1 John Henry was a little boy,
No bigger than the palm of your hand,
By the time that boy was nine years old,
He was hammering spikes[1] like a man,
He was hammering spikes like a man.

2 John Henry said to the captain,
"A man is nothing but a man,
But before I let the steam drill beat[2] me down,
I'm going to die with a hammer in my hand,
Die with a hammer in my hand."

3 John Henry said to the captain, yeah,
"Man, you ought to see me swing,
I'm not going to let that steam drill beat me down,
Love to hear the cold steel ring,[3]
Love to hear the cold steel ring."

4 John Henry went into that tunnel,
Steam drill was by his side,
He beat that steam drill with three inches to spare,
Then he laid down his hammer and he died,
Laid down a hammer and he died.

5 They took John Henry to the graveyard,[4]
Buried him in six feet of sand,
Each time a train engine passes by,
It says, "There lies a steel hammering man,
There lies a steel hammering man."

[1]**spikes:** metal rods
[2]**beat:** win a race
[3]**ring:** the sound of the metal hammer hitting the metal rod
[4]**graveyard:** place where dead people are buried

Although John Henry is a fictional hero, the story in the song is based in fact. After the Civil War in the United States, many of the freed slaves worked building railroads. To make the tunnels, the workers had to drill holes in the mountain. They put explosives in the holes. That is how they opened the rock to make tunnels. Making tunnels was very hard work. The workers sang songs to make the work easier.

Making an Oral Presentation

At some time, you will need to give a presentation in English to a small audience. At work, you might have to teach co-workers about something you know. In class, you will often have to make a short speech. Now you will give a short speech in class about your personal hero.

Most people feel nervous when they talk to a group. Do you feel nervous? Here are some steps you can take to relax:

1. Prepare your ideas before you speak.

2. Practice, practice, practice. Some people like to practice in front of a mirror so they can see what they look like.

3. Take a deep breath before you start to speak.

4. Remember that everyone feels nervous. Your teachers feel nervous, too!

You will give a short presentation to your classmates. Take time now to prepare your ideas before you speak. In your presentation you should tell these things:

1. Who your hero is.

2. Why he or she is your hero.

3. What he or she is like (give a description).

4. What his or her accomplishments are.

Remember to elaborate on your answers. Add details, information, and examples to make them more interesting.

Practice your speech with a partner.

Presenting

Take turns giving your presentation to your classmates. Remember to take a deep breath right before you start speaking!

Make a chart like this one. Take notes on your classmates' speeches using this chart:

	Speaker	Hero	Description	Accomplishments
1				
2				
3				
4				

After the presentations, your teacher might give you a quiz about what you heard. You can use your notes to answer the questions on the quiz.

Evaluate Your Performance

How did you feel during your speech? When were you the most nervous? Before you started or after you started? What can you do next time to feel more comfortable?

ACADEMIC POWER STRATEGY

Apply the Strategy

Find a mentor who can help you be successful in school. A *mentor* is a person who you can learn from. He or she is often an older or more experienced person. A mentor helps you and teaches you. A mentor can be anyone you admire that you can learn from.

Think about the people you know who inspire you. Write their names here:

_____

_____

_____

Now think about how you can learn from them. Choose one of these ways. Do it this week.

1. Interview the person about his or her life and profession.

2. Ask the person to spend some time with you. Talk to him or her about your dreams and goals. Ask your mentor for advice.

3. Teachers make good mentors. Make an appointment with a teacher and ask the teacher for advice on how you can improve in your classes.

4. Make an appointment with an academic counselor. Ask the counselor for advice about your academic life.

Who is your personal hero? Write about him or her.

1. Describe him or her.

2. Explain why he or she is your hero.

EXAMPLE:

When I was young, my hero was John Lennon. I still enjoy listening to his music. The songs and lyrics he wrote are still popular today. I also like John Lennon because he was creative and independent. He tried to do different things with his music. All of the girls liked him because he was handsome. John had great style. He was a good father. He stayed at home with his son, Sean. It's too bad that he died so young. We might have more songs by John Lennon today.

_____

_____

_____

_____

_____

PUTTING IT ALL TOGETHER

Your teacher may assign one or all of the activities below:

Your Favorite Song

Do you have a favorite song in English? Share your favorite song with your classmates. You can bring a recording of the song or sing it to your classmates. Make a copy of the words so your classmates can sing the song with you or your recording.

Hero Songs

Here are some more songs about heroes. Find a recording of the songs and learn them.

"Wind Beneath My Wings," performed by Bette Midler

"Billy Don't Be a Hero," performed by Bo Donaldson & The Heywoods

"Hero," performed by Mariah Carey

Research Report

Find out more information about one of the heroes mentioned in this chapter. Tell your classmates the new information you learned.

 **Who Is a Hero?**

With your classmates, discuss these questions. Practice giving interesting answers:

- What is the difference between a hero and a celebrity?
- Are all of the people mentioned in this chapter heroes?
- Do heroes have to be perfect role models?

Test-Taking Tip

Before you begin the test, read all the directions carefully. Also, listen for any additional instructions your teacher may give just before the test begins. If there is anything in the instructions that you don't understand, don't panic. Ask your teacher to explain. Understanding the directions completely will help you feel confident and focused as you begin the test.

CHECK YOUR PROGRESS

On a scale of 1 to 5, rate how well you have mastered the goals set at the beginning of the chapter:

1 2 3 4 5   use a chart to help you take good notes when you listen.

1 2 3 4 5   describe people's personalities.

1 2 3 4 5   use adjectives to make descriptions.

1 2 3 4 5   pronounce the long *e* sound correctly.

1 2 3 4 5   elaborate on your answers.

1 2 3 4 5   use music to help you learn English and improve your pronunciation.

1 2 3 4 5   find a mentor.

If you've given yourself a 3 or lower on any of these goals:

- visit the *Tapestry* web site for additional practice.
- ask your instructor for extra help.
- review the sections of the chapter that you found difficult.
- work with a partner or study group to further your progress.

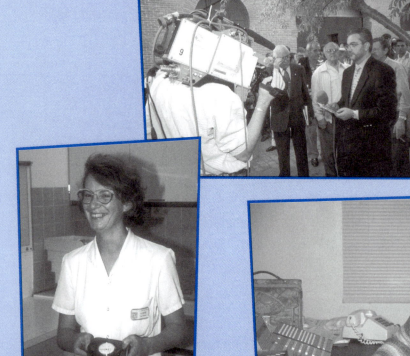

L ook at the photos. Discuss these questions with your
classmates:

• What kind of jobs do you think these people do?

• Which people work inside?

• Which people work outside?

• Do they look happy at their work?

• Do any of these jobs interest you?

Tell a partner which jobs are most interesting to you and why
they are interesting.

GET A JOB!

One of the first questions that English speakers often ask when they meet someone new is "What do you do?" Of course, this means "What kind of work do you do?" or "What job do you have?" The kind of work you do is important information for people from the United States and Canada.

Unless you are already a millionaire, you will have to work in order to have money to live. However, deciding on a career is not always easy. First you have to decide what career is best for you. Then you have to find out what kind of training or education you need to get the job you want. This chapter has information about different kinds of jobs and what kind of education is necessary for each job.

Setting Goals

In this chapter you will learn:

◆ to focus on content words to improve your understanding when you listen.

◆ how to talk about habits and routines.

◆ how to pronounce *s* three different ways.

◆ to group words by type and meaning.

◆ how to make a career plan.

◆ to fill out a job application.

◆ how to give formal and informal answers to questions.

◆ to ask questions in English.

◆ to prepare for a job interview.

183

◆**Getting Started**

Work with a partner. Which of these job titles are new to you? Check the ones you know. Which of these jobs require the most education? Why? Which job do you think earns the most money? What are the advantages and disadvantages of each job?

_____ nurse   _____ elementary school teacher

_____ X-ray technician   _____ receptionist

_____ professional athlete   _____ accountant

_____ mechanic   _____ news reporter

_____ bus driver   _____ firefighter

PART 1: The World of Work

How many different kinds of jobs can you think of? Work with a partner to make a list of different kinds of jobs. Compare your list with your classmates. Which of the jobs are new to you? Which jobs did you know about already?

LANGUAGE LEARNING STRATEGY

Focus on content words to improve your understanding when you listen. It is easier to understand what you hear if you first focus on the words that carry the central meaning, or the content words. There are many ways to learn content words. Pictures, photos, written clues, and the body language of a speaker can give you clues about the meaning of new words. You do not have to understand every word all of the time. Once you understand the main idea of a message, the details are easier to learn.

Apply the Strategy

Look at the photos and read the words. Circle the words in each sentence that are content words (words that carry the central meaning).

◆**Getting Ready to Listen**

With a partner, discuss which words you circled as content words. Did you both circle the same words? When you listen to the tape, pay special attention to the content words.

Listen

Listening 1: Talking About Work

As you listen to the tape, check all of the statements that are true.

Felix

_____ He works in an office.

_____ He knows how to type.

_____ He writes reports for his boss.

_____ People ask Felix for appointments.

_____ He doesn't like his job.

_____ He finishes work at the same time every day.

Felix is a receptionist.

Claudia

_____ She starts work at the same time every day.

_____ Claudia stays in shape by jogging and swimming.

_____ Being in good shape is important in her job.

_____ Claudia likes her job.

_____ She thinks her job is important.

_____ Sometimes she helps injured people.

Claudia is a firefighter.

Bernice

_____ Bernice only works at night.

_____ The restaurant is usually busy.

_____ She has an easy job.

_____ Bernice works hard.

_____ She gets tired at work.

_____ She likes her job.

Bernice is a server.

After You Listen

Compare your answers with a partner. Are your answers the same? Talk about Bernice, Claudia, and Felix with your partner. Whose job do you think is the best? Why?

LANGUAGE YOU CAN USE: TALKING ABOUT HABITS AND ROUTINES

Habits and routines are things that you usually do. When you talk about things people usually do, use simple present tense verbs. Don't forget to add an *s* to the verb when the subject is *he, she,* or *it*. What are some things that you usually do?

USING NEW LANGUAGE

Look at the photos. Do you know the people in the photos? What jobs do these people do? Work with a partner. Using the cue words, tell your partner what each person does in his or her job.

1. Bobbi McCaughy is a mother.

have eight children

take care of her children

cook food

feed the babies

clean house

read her children stories

Eighty-five percent of all jobs in the United States require education beyond high school. Technical schools, colleges, universities, and special training programs in large corporations provide this education.

2. Jackie Chan is an action movie hero.

make movies

catch bad guys

use martial arts

make people laugh

3. Prince William and Prince Harry are students.

go to school

study

read books

write papers

play soccer

4. Ricky Martin is a singer.

sing

dance

make recordings

5. Penn and Teller are magicians.

do magic tricks

tell jokes

entertain people

6. Mark McGuire is a baseball player.

throw balls

catch balls

hit home runs

7. Cokie Roberts is a reporter.

work in Washington, D.C.

report news

interview politicians

8. Bill Gates is a businessperson.

own Microsoft

sell computer software

run a big company

More Practice

Play a game with your classmates. Think of a famous person or job. Tell your classmates some of the things the person does. Your classmates must guess the person or job. For example:

He works in a big office. He lives in a white house. He visits other countries. He signs bills. Who is he? (the president of the United States)

The Sound of It: Three Different Ways to Say *s*

Listen very carefully as your teacher reads this sentence:

Shelly watches, listens, and waits.

Listen again. Did you notice that the *s* on the end of each verb is pronounced differently? Now try to say the sentence. Pay special attention to the sound at the end of the word.

How It Works

Why are there three different ways to pronounce *s*? The way you pronounce *s* at the end of a word depends on the sounds that come before it.

Ending sound	Sound of *s*	Examples
k, p, t, f, or *th*	/s/ (as in likes)	talks, sleeps, meets
x, z, ss, ch, or *sh*	/iz/ (as in watches)	boxes, wishes, kisses
all other sounds	/z/ in zoo	tells, hides, goes, does

Listen to these words. Write them under the correct sound. The first one has been done for you as an example.

works	lives	teaches	helps	cooks	washes
makes	buys	sells	phones	keeps	fixes
drives	watches	does	builds	delivers	treats
prices	thinks	repairs	sees	takes	reads

/s/	/iz/	/z/
1. works	1.	1.
2.	2.	2.
3.	3.	3.
4.	4.	4.
5.	5.	5.
6.		6.
7.		7.
8.		8.
		9.
		10.
		11.

Pronunciation Practice

Make sentences by matching the jobs with the activities. Say the sentences. Pay attention to the pronunciation of the final *s* sound.
For example, you say "A mechanic repairs cars."

A doctor   . . . repairs cars.

A sales clerk   . . . treats patients.

A mechanic   . . . helps people get well.

. . . counts money.

. . . reads a medical record.

. . . fixes engines.

. . . writes a prescription.

. . . gives change.

. . . keeps a medical record.

. . . phones customers.

. . . gives patients advice on how to stay healthy.

. . . answers questions from customers.

. . . listens to patients.

. . . checks for mechanical problems.

. . . sells products.

. . . puts price tags on merchandise.

. . . talks to customers.

. . . reads a medical book.

More Practice

Practice this exercise again with a partner. Listen to your partner say each sentence. Does your partner pronounce the *s* sound correctly? If you want more practice, do the speaking exercise on pages 188–189 again. Pronounce the verbs carefully.

LANGUAGE LEARNING STRATEGY

A fun way to practice difficult sounds is to say tongue twisters. Tongue twisters are sentences with many similar sounds. One famous tongue twister in English is "Peter Piper picked a peck of pickled peppers." Because the sounds of the words are similar, you have to say the sentence slowly to pronounce the words correctly. Do you have tongue twisters in your first language?

Apply the Strategy

Say this tongue twister aloud. It will help you pronounce the different sounds of *s*.

Shelly works in a stationery shop. All week she stocks the shelves and sells stationery. On Sundays, she sits by the sea. Shelly watches, listens, and waits for the seals to show up.

Many teenagers in the United States work part time while they go to high school. They do not work because their families are poor; they work so they can have some money of their own to spend. Many parents encourage their teenagers to work. They believe that having a job when you are young makes you a more responsible adult.

◆Grouping Words by Type

In this exercise, you will practice grouping words in different ways. This will help you remember the new words.

Notice that many words that you use to describe professions end in the same letters. The endings *or, er, ist,* and *ian* mean a person who does something. For example, an editor is a person who edits, a writer is a person who writes, a typist is a person who types, and a musician is a person who plays music.

Put these professions in the correct column. The first one has been done for you as an example: **Doctor,** Professional Athlete, Elementary School Teacher, Business Administator, Medical Records Transcriber, Truck Driver, Mail Carrier, College Professor, Accountant, Actress, Dispatcher, Secondary School Teacher, Dentist, Marketing Specialist, Comedian, Principal, Nurse, Firefighter, Corporate Trainer, Police Officer, Physical Therapist, Dancer, Actor, Bus Driver, Musician, Taxi Driver, Corrections Officer, Librarian, Pilot, Bank Teller, Auditor.

(Exercise continues on next page)

"or"	"ist"	"ian"
1. Doctor	**1.**	**1.**
2.	**2.**	**2.**
3.	**3.**	**3.**
4.		
5.		

<table>
<tr><td>"er"</td><td></td><td>others</td></tr>
<tr><td>1.</td><td>8.</td><td>1.</td></tr>
<tr><td>2.</td><td>9.</td><td>2.</td></tr>
<tr><td>3.</td><td>10.</td><td>3.</td></tr>
<tr><td>4.</td><td>11.</td><td>4.</td></tr>
<tr><td>5.</td><td>12.</td><td>5.</td></tr>
<tr><td>6.</td><td>13.</td><td>6.</td></tr>
<tr><td>7.</td><td>14.</td><td></td></tr>
</table>

◆ Grouping Words by Meaning

Another way to group words is by meaning. This will help you remember related words.

Finish these lists by putting the careers in the correct categories. If you do not know the meaning of a word, look it up in your dictionary, then put it in the correct category. The first one has been done for you: **Doctor**, Professional Athlete, Elementary School Teacher, Business Administator, Medical Records Transcriber, Truck Driver, Mail Carrier, College Professor, Accountant, Actress, Dispatcher, Secondary School Teacher, Dentist, Marketing Specialist, Comedian, Principal, Nurse, Firefighter, Corporate Trainer, Police Officer, Physical Therapist, Dancer, Actor, Bus Driver, Musician, Taxi Driver, Corrections Officer, Librarian, Pilot, Bank Teller, Auditor.

<table>
<tr>
<td>

Medical Careers

1. Doctor
2.
3.
4.
5.
6.

</td>
<td>

Education Careers

1.
2.
3.
4.
5.
6.

</td>
<td>

Entertainers

1.
2.
3.
4.
5.
6.

</td>
</tr>
<tr>
<td>

Business Careers

1.
2.
3.
4.
5.

</td>
<td>

Transportation Careers

1.
2.
3.
4.
5.

</td>
<td>

Public Service Careers

1.
2.
3.

</td>
</tr>
</table>

When they first meet you, North Americans usually ask "What do you do?" The expected answer to this question is your career or job. For example, you can answer the question "What do you do?" by saying "I'm a student" or "I'm a cashier" or "I work at a restaurant."

 Brainstorming

Some jobs have too many qualified workers, while other jobs do not have enough qualified workers. With your classmates, think of as many jobs in each category as possible.

TOO MANY WORKERS	TOO FEW WORKERS
_____	_____
_____	_____
_____	_____
_____	_____
_____	_____

TUNING IN: "Tech Worker Shortage"

This video tells about a type of job that does not have enough qualified workers. Before you watch the videotape, look at the phrases below. Put a check mark (✓) by the phrases you know already. Put a question mark (?) by the phrases you are not sure of. Watch the video. Listen for these phrases. Guess the meanings of the words or phrases you did not know. Compare your guesses with a partner. Check your guesses with a dictionary or with your teacher.

© CNN

_____ high-tech workers   _____ poacher   _____ job fair

_____ résumé   _____ out of town   _____ annual

_____ electrical engineering   _____ right out of college

 **Listening Activity**

1. Listen for the number of job openings at various tech companies attending the job fair:

COMPANY REPRESENTATIVE	NUMBER OF JOB OPENINGS
Blond woman with glasses.	_____
Young man in tie.	_____
Brunette woman with glasses.	_____
Woman wearing a white shirt.	_____
Woman with short, blond hair.	_____

2. What were the reactions of people who were looking for jobs?

Think About It

Which of these things do you think is most important to consider when choosing a career? Explain your choices.

1. There are many jobs available.

2. It is what you enjoy doing.

3. It is what your parents want you to do.

4. It is a high-paid job.

PART 2: Make a Career Plan

You can't just let your career happen. You've got to plan for it. In this section you'll find out how to make a career plan.

ACADEMIC POWER STRATEGY

Make a career plan to help you prepare for the future. If you have a plan to reach your goals, you are more likely to be successful. A plan shows you how much time it will take you to complete your career goal. Making a career plan is one of the basic steps in planning for your future.

Apply the Strategy

The first step to making a career plan is to think of different careers that interest you. Make a list of three careers that you find interesting:

1. _____

2. _____

3. _____

Share your list with a partner. Tell your partner why you think these careers are interesting.

 Getting Ready to Listen

The following chart uses content words to show the main steps in making a career plan. However, some words are missing. Read the chart carefully. Use a dictionary to look up any content words that you don't know. Listen to the tape once while you look at the chart. Then listen to it again. Fill in the content words that are missing. Don't worry about understanding everything. Just try to get the main idea of the tape.

 Listen

Listening 2: A Career Plan

Women in the United States are generally expected to train for a career. About 60% of women in the United States work outside of their home. Women now work at more jobs that have traditionally been men's jobs. Women are presidents of companies. They fight fires, work on construction sites, and deliver mail. Because of this, the traditional names of these jobs have been changed. For example firemen are now called "firefighters," mailmen are called "mail carriers," and policemen are called "police officers." Men also do some jobs that were traditionally women's jobs. For example, more men are nurses and elementary school teachers.

Steps in Making a Career Plan

Here are some easy _____ to follow to plan your career. If you follow these steps carefully, you will be successful.

1. Do a Self-Assessment:

First, you should do a _____. A self-assessment is a way to find out about yourself. A self-assessment helps you find out about your interests, _____, and personality. You can do this by taking a formal _____, or by writing down the things you like to do and the things that you are good at.

2. Gather Information About Different Occupations:

Second, you should gather information about different occupations. There are many books and _____ that tell about different jobs. Find these books and _____ them. Who knows? You may find out about a job that you did not know existed. You should also talk to _____ about different kinds of jobs. Talk to people who are doing the job you are interested in, or talk to your teacher or _____ at school. The _____ and people can help you find out two important things: how much time it will take to study for your _____ and what is the best way to get the _____ you need. This will also help you decide if you have the time and the _____ to reach your career goal.

3. Get the Skills You Need:

The third thing you have to do is to get the _____

you need. You can do this by getting more education at a

_____, university, or technical _____ or by

learning on the job.

4. Learn How to Find a Job:

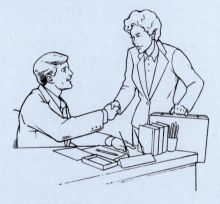

The final step is to learn _____ to find a job.

Once you finish your _____, you cannot sit and

wait for jobs to come to you. You must show what you know in a

job _____. You also need to present yourself in a

_____.

After You Listen   Compare your notes with your partner. Do you have the answers?
Listen to the tape again and check your answers.

Pair Activity   Think about the steps in a career plan. Then talk about these questions with a partner. Have you done any of these steps already?
What do you need to do? What are you doing right now?

Do a Self-Assessment

Read this self-assessment test. Do you understand all of the words?
Ask a classmate about the words you don't understand, or look up
the words in a dictionary. Read the list again. Check those activities
you like to do or think you would like to do. Check those activities
you don't like to do or don't care about.

	LIKE	DON'T LIKE
Fix electrical appliances	_____	_____
Repair cars	_____	_____
Build things with wood	_____	_____
Hunt or fish	_____	_____
Take a class on how to build things	_____	_____
Total Likes (Section A)	_____	
Read science books	_____	_____
Work in a laboratory	_____	_____
Work on a science project	_____	_____
Use math to solve problems	_____	_____
Take a biology class	_____	_____
Total Likes (Section B)	_____	
Draw or paint	_____	_____
Act in a play	_____	_____
Read or write poetry	_____	_____
Write for a magazine	_____	_____
Practice a musical instrument	_____	_____
Total Likes (Section C)	_____	
Teach things to people	_____	_____
Do volunteer work	_____	_____
Take a psychology class	_____	_____
Take care of children	_____	_____
Help others with their problems	_____	_____
Total Likes (Section D)	_____	

	LIKE	DON'T LIKE
Sell something	_____	_____
Run your own business	_____	_____
Supervise other workers	_____	_____
Meet with business and political leaders	_____	_____
Lead a group	_____	_____
Total Likes (Section E)	_____	
Fill out tax forms	_____	_____
Type letters or papers	_____	_____
Use a computer	_____	_____
Use math skills	_____	_____
Take a business class	_____	_____
Total Likes (Section F)	_____	

Add the totals in each section. Which sections have the most Likes?

Talk About the Self-Assessment

Work with a partner. Tell your partner what things you like to do. Look at the jobs that go with each section. Have you heard of these jobs? If you're not sure what they are, look them up in a dictionary or ask your teacher. Do you think these are good jobs for you?

SECTION A	SECTION B	SECTION C
Airplane Mechanic	Meteorologist	Musician
Carpenter	Medical Lab Technician	Actor/Actress
Construction Worker	Biologist	Journalist
Electrician	Zoologist	Cartoonist
SECTION D	**SECTION E**	**SECTION F**
Teacher	Entrepreneur	Bookkeeper
Social Worker	Travel Guide	Bank Teller
Youth Camp Director	Salesperson	Credit Investigator
Psychologist	Purchasing Agent	Business Teacher

Compare the list of jobs from the previous page with the list you made in the Academic Power Strategy on page 195. Did the self-assessment help you think of other jobs? Can you think of other jobs that go in each section?

Talk About It

Look again at the list of jobs on page 199. Work in a group of three or four students. Each group will be responsible for one of the sections. With your group members, make a list of the different things a person with that job would do. Try to think of at least five sentences for each job. For example, you might say:

"An airplane mechanic repairs planes." "She works at the airport." "She knows about jet engines."

After you talk about each job on your list, share your sentences with another group. Make sure each person in your group gets a chance to talk about at least one job. Be careful with the pronunciation of the final *s*.

Getting Ready to Read

Jobs that require math and science have increased by 36% since 1986. These include jobs in health care, business, and computer technology.

Talking about a reading selection before you read helps you understand more of what you read. Talk about this reading selection before you read it. Employers were asked what skills and qualities they think are most important for their employees. What do you think would be the most important? Before you read "Ten Most Important Skills and Qualities for Work," guess what the employers said. With a partner, make a list of the five most important skills and qualities to be a good worker. For example, you might think one of the most important skills for work is this: Get along with co-workers. (Do this exercise without looking at the list on page 201.)

Five Most Important Skills and Qualities for Work

1. _____

2. _____

3. _____

4. _____

5. _____

When you finish, do the following activities:

1. Each group in your class should tell your teacher the five skills they think are most important.

2. Your teacher will write each group's list on the board. If there are any that are the same, your teacher will count how many are similar. You and your classmates can group qualities that are similar.

3. Choose the ten most frequent skills from your class list.

4. Compare your list to the employers' list below.

Read

Ten Most Important Skills and Qualities for Work

1. Problem Solving: the ability to suggest several answers to a problem and make a plan to fix it.
2. Research Skills: the ability to find information from different resources, such as books, computers, co-workers, or other people.
3. Organization: the ability to do things systematically without wasting time or energy. Also, the ability to put things away neatly.
4. Verbal Skills: the ability to speak clearly in English.
5. Writing Skills: the ability to use correct spelling and grammar. Also, the ability to organize ideas when writing.
6. Ability to Work with Others: the ability to get along with people, to work with people of different ages and from different places.
7. Mathematical and Analytical Skills: the ability to understand the basic concepts of mathematics (add, subtract, multiply, divide, use fractions and percentage). Also, the ability to use scientific processes.
8. Ethical: truthful and honest.
9. Technological Skills: the ability to use computers and other technology, or willingness to learn to use computers and other technology.
10. Flexibility: the willingness to try and learn new and different things. Also, the desire to improve yourself by learning new things.

After you Read

Look at the predictions your class made. Which skills are the same as the list the employers made? Which are different?

Vocabulary Building

Did you understand all of the words in the reading? Check your comprehension. Complete the crossword puzzle on the next page.

Across

2. In good order

5. Algebra, for example

7. A truthful person has strong
   _____.

8. Not messy

9. Always tell the truth

Down

1. Try new and different things

3. For example: $\frac{1}{2}$

4. %

6. Find the answer

 **Working in a Group**

Work in a small group of three to five students. Assign these three roles to three members of the group. Make sure that each member understands each role. Look back at Chapter 4 if you need a reminder on how to work successfully in a group.

Roles

Facilitator: The facilitator makes sure each group member speaks for the same amount of time. He or she makes sure all the group members are heard.

Recorder: The recorder write down notes on what the group members say. The recorder fills in the chart.

Summarizer: The summarizer uses the notes the recorder wrote down. He or she tells the whole class the main points of the discussion.

Decide which of the ten skills would be most important for each of the different careers below. Choose the best answer based on what all the members of the group think.

EXAMPLE: I think math and science skills are most important for being a nurse. A nurse needs to know about biology and medicine. A nurse needs to have good math skills to figure out how much medicine to give a patient.

PROFESSION	MOST IMPORTANT SKILL	WHY?
1. Nurse		
2. Cashier		
3. Corrections Officer		
4. Dietician		
5. Flight Attendant		
6. Lawyer		

PART 3: Get a Job

Can you write an employment application? Have you ever had a job interview? This section will help you practice these skills.

Look at the questions on the employment application. Do you know all of the information on the application? What will you need to find out before you fill out the application?

Employment Application

PERSONAL

Name (Last name, first name) _____

Street Address _____

City, State, Zip code _____

Phone Number _____

Social Security Number _____ — _____ — _____

EDUCATION

	Years Attended	Degree or Diploma
High School _____	_____	_____
Higher Education _____	_____	_____
_____	_____	_____

WORK EXPERIENCE

Employer _____ Reason for leaving _____

Title _____ Phone Number _____ Years Employed _____

Employer _____ Reason for leaving _____

Title _____ Phone Number _____ Years Employed _____

Employer _____ Reason for leaving _____

Title _____ Phone Number _____ Years Employed _____

What is the position that you are applying for? Explain why you think you would be a good person for this job: _____

_____

_____

Check your application. Did you answer all the questions? Did you write your answers neatly? Would this application impress an employer? Exchange applications with a partner and discuss how the applications can be improved.

More Practice

What is your dream job? Write a paragraph describing your dream job. Share your paragraph with your classmates.

LANGUAGE YOU CAN USE: FORMAL AND INFORMAL ANSWERS

You should use short answers when speaking, except in formal situations. In spoken English, it is normal to answer questions with a short answer. However, in formal situations, you should answer questions completely.

USING NEW LANGUAGE

> **Work is life, you know, and without it, there's nothing but fear and insecurity.**
>
> **—JOHN LENNON**

Look at each of these situations. Decide if they are formal or informal. (There may be different opinions about some of these situations.) Choose the short or long answer for each situation. Compare your answers with a partner. Explain why you chose a short or long answer.

Your teacher asks you: Is your group ready to make a presentation?
Yes, we are.   Yes, we are ready to present.

A judge asks you: Where were you when the accident happened?
On the corner.   I was standing on the corner.

Your friend asks you: Would you like to see a movie this weekend?
Sure!   Yes, I would like to see a movie.

In a job interview you are asked: Can you work on weekends?
Yeah.   Yes, I can work on weekends.

Your mother asks you: When will you clean your room?
I'll do it right now.   I'll clean my room right now.

Practicing saying these questions and answers. When would you use the short answer? When would you use the long answer? Circle the subject of each sentence. Underline the verb, or verbs, in each sentence. How does the order of the words change when you ask a question?

QUESTION	SHORT ANSWER	LONG ANSWER
Is she a lawyer?	Yes, she is.	Yes, she is a lawyer.
Is her office downtown?	No, it isn't.	No, her office is not downtown. It is near the courthouse.
Are they lawyers too?	No, they aren't.	No, they are not lawyers. They are legal secretaries.
Are they working on a new case?	Yes, they are.	Yes, they are working on a new case.
Does he work in a law office?	Yes, he does.	Yes, he works in a law office.
Do they have law books?	Yes, they do.	Yes, they have law books.
Do they work on Saturday?	No, they don't.	No, they do not work on Saturday.
Can you work at the courthouse?	No, I can't.	No, I cannot work at the courthouse. I'm not a lawyer.

 **More Practice**

Work with a partner. Look at these photos. Using the cues, ask yes/no questions about the photos. Your partner will answer the questions with short answers. Then answer your partner's questions. The first one has been done for you as an example.

COMPUTER PROGRAMMER

Cecil/work outdoors/make a lot of money

Example:

A: Is Cecil a computer programmer?   B: Yes, he is.

A: Does a computer programmer work outdoors?   B: No, he doesn't.

A: Can a computer programmer make a lot of money? B: Yes, he can. OR I don't know.

PARK RANGER

Roberta/work outdoors/drive a truck/make a lot of money/repair cars

TRAVEL AGENT

Yandy and Thomas/make reservations/plan a trip/serve food/
work long hours

HOUSE PAINTER

Siu/paint car/make a lot of money/get messy/work outside

PLUMBER

Domonic/repair a lamp/work on Saturday/fix a shower/fix a sink

FLIGHT ATTENDANT

Jie/help passengers/fly an airplane/work on Sunday/
work outside/speak several languages

LANGUAGE YOU CAN USE: INFORMATION QUESTIONS

The word order in information questions is similar to yes/no questions. However, information questions begin with a question word. Practice by saying these examples aloud:

Question	Answer
Where is your application?	It's right here.
How are you?	I'm fine.
Why do you want this job?	Because I like to help people.
Where do I leave this application?	Right here. I can take it for you.
When does the job start?	On Monday.
What kind of job are you looking for?	I'm looking for a cashier's position.
When can you start?	I can start right now, if you want.
How many hours can she work?	She can work four hours per day.
Who is the boss?*	Mr. Murphy is the boss.
Who can fix this problem?*	I can fix it.

*Notice that questions that start with *who* are a little different because they ask about the subject of the sentence. *Who* replaces the subject of the sentence.

USING NEW LANGUAGE

To get a job in North America, most people must have a job interview. A job interview is when the employer asks someone who wants a job some questions about himself or herself. In this activity, you will work with a small group to do a role play. One of the members of your group will be the boss. The rest of the group will be people who want a job. The boss will ask questions. The other group members will try to answer the questions in a way that will convince the boss to hire them.

Here are the job notices posted on the bulletin board at your school:

Positions Available

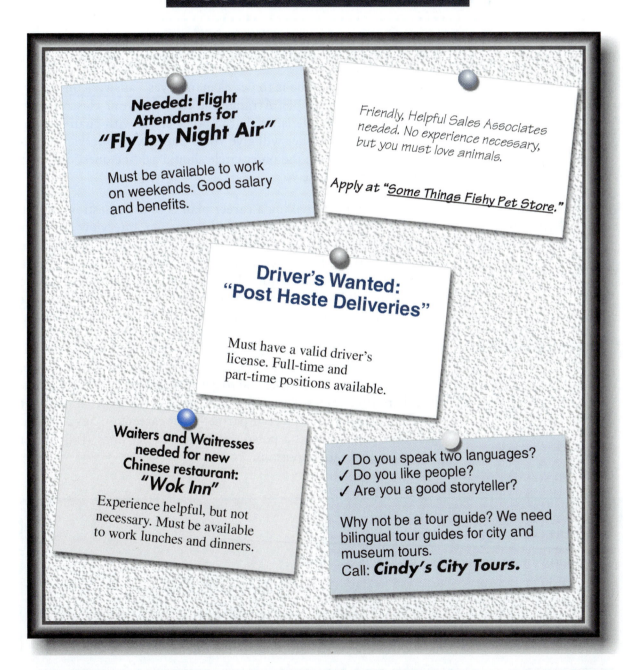

Needed: Flight Attendants for "Fly by Night Air"

Must be available to work on weekends. Good salary and benefits.

Friendly, Helpful Sales Associates needed. No experience necessary, but you must love animals.

Apply at "Some Things Fishy Pet Store."

Driver's Wanted: "Post Haste Deliveries"

Must have a valid driver's license. Full-time and part-time positions available.

Waiters and Waitresses needed for new Chinese restaurant: "Wok Inn"

Experience helpful, but not necessary. Must be available to work lunches and dinners.

✓ Do you speak two languages?
✓ Do you like people?
✓ Are you a good storyteller?

Why not be a tour guide? We need bilingual tour guides for city and museum tours.
Call: **Cindy's City Tours.**

Practice your role play several times; then present it to your classmates. Listen to each group's presentation. Decide who you think would make the best employee in each group. Compare your choice with your other classmates. Explain why that person was the best candidate.

PUTTING IT ALL TOGETHER

Your teacher may assign one or all of the activities below:

◆ **Ask Around**

The object of this game is to get as many "yes" answers on the interview sheet as possible. Arrange the chairs in your classroom in two circles. One circle is inside the other circle with chairs facing each other. Your teacher will give you a paper with interview questions. The students in the outer circle should ask the questions first. Your teacher will time you.

◆ **Interview People About Their Work**

One of the steps in making a career plan is to ask questions about different careers. By yourself or with a partner, interview a person about the job he or she does. Plan what questions you will ask. Be sure to ask about his or her duties. Also, ask him or her about the training and education required for the job. Ask him or her advice for getting a job. Thank the person for the interview. Report what you found out to your classmates.

◆ **Make Your Career Plan**

Write a career plan. Include (1) the job you want to have, (2) the education you need to get that job, (3) the skills you want to improve, and (4) how long it will take you to get the education. When you finish, share your career plan with a partner. Ask questions about your partner's career plan. Tell your partner what career you have chosen. Tell your partner what a person with that career does. Talk about why your goals are important.

Test-Taking Tip

Improve your performance on True/False tests:

- Read carefully—sometimes one word can make an answer wrong.
- Pay attention to important words—*all, most, sometimes, never,* and *rarely* are key words.
- If the question contains the words *always* or *never,* it is usually false.

CHECK YOUR PROGRESS

On a scale of 1 to 5, rate how well you have mastered the goals set at the beginning of the chapter:

1 2 3 4 5 focus on content words to improve your under-standing when you listen.

1 2 3 4 5 talk about habits and routines.

1 2 3 4 5 pronounce *s* three different ways.

1 2 3 4 5 group words by type and meaning.

1 2 3 4 5 make a career plan.

1 2 3 4 5 fill out a job application.

1 2 3 4 5 give formal and informal answers to questions.

1 2 3 4 5 ask questions in English.

1 2 3 4 5 prepare for a job interview.

If you've given yourself a 3 or lower on any of these goals:

- visit the *Tapestry* web site for additional practice.
- ask your instructor for extra help.
- review the sections of the chapter that you found difficult.
- work with a partner or study group to further your progress.

This is a picture of a nuclear family.

This is a picture of an extended family.

- Which type of family, nuclear or extended, is most like your family? Explain how.

- Which type of family, nuclear or extended, is most common in your native culture?

ALL IN THE FAMILY

In this chapter, you will talk about family. You will think about the many ways in which families are important. You will both hear and tell family stories. You will also discuss pets, an important part of many families in the United States and Canada. In this chapter, it's all in the family!

Setting Goals

In this chapter you will learn to:

◈ ask about and give information about families.

◈ predict what you will hear.

◈ use time expressions to tell a story.

◈ pronounce simple past *-ed* endings correctly.

◈ repeat new words and phrases several times.

◈ talk about responsibilities.

◈ make a schedule to use your time well.

**Getting Started**

This is a family tree. A family tree shows the relationships between members of a family. This one is missing some family members. Work with a partner and fill in the missing family members.

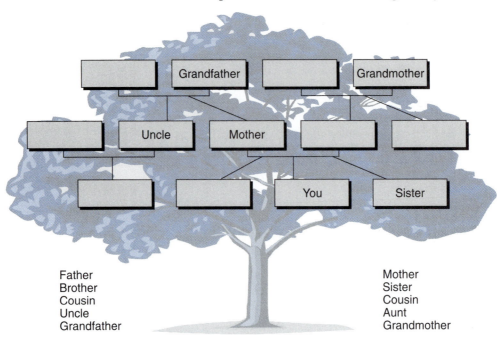

	Grandfather		Grandmother

| | Uncle | Mother | | |

| | | | You | Sister |

Father
Brother
Cousin
Uncle
Grandfather

Mother
Sister
Cousin
Aunt
Grandmother

PART 1: Family Members

LANGUAGE YOU CAN USE: ASKING AND GIVING INFORMATION ABOUT FAMILY

ASKING ABOUT FAMILY

How many people are there in your family?

Where does your family live?

Do you have any siblings?

Do you have any children?

How many aunts and uncles do you have?

Are you married?

GIVING INFORMATION ABOUT FAMILY

There are ten people in my family.
There are six of us.

My family lives in Malaysia.
They live in Florida.

I have one sister and four brothers.
I'm an only child.

I don't have any children.

I have one aunt and two uncles on my mother's side and two uncles on my father's side.

No, I'm single.
Yes, I have a husband.
No, I'm divorced.

USING NEW LANGUAGE

Interview a classmate about his or her family. Use the expressions on the previous page and take notes. Tell your class about your partner's family.

◀ **Getting Ready to Listen**

LANGUAGE LEARNING STRATEGY

Predict what you will hear before you listen. Good listeners predict or guess what they will hear. When you predict, you start to think about the topic. This helps you understand what you hear. It can also help you focus while you listen. Then you can check your predictions as you listen. All predictions are good, even if they aren't correct.

Apply the Strategy

You will hear two people talk about their families. Makiko is from Japan, and Juan is from Mexico. Before you listen, predict what they will say about their families. Write *T* if you think the statement will be true. Write *F* if you think the statement will be false. Compare your answers with a classmate.

_____ Makiko has many siblings.

_____ Juan is an only child.

_____ Makiko's grandmother lives with her family.

_____ There are eleven people in Juan's family.

_____ Makiko's family is small.

_____ Juan's family is small.

◀ **Listen**

Listening 1: Talking About Family

Choose the correct answer.

Part 1

1. There are _____ people in Makiko's family.

   a. four

   b. five

2. Makiko has one _____.

   a. sister

   b. brother

3. Makiko's _____ lives with her family.

   a. grandmother

   b. grandfather

Part 2

4. Juan's family is _____.

   a. pretty small

   b. pretty big

5. Juan has three _____.

   a. brothers

   b. sisters

6. Juan's grandparents live with his _____.

   a. aunt

   b. uncle

7. There are _____ people in Juan's family.

   a. ten

   b. eleven

> The Family Economics Research Group of the U.S. Department of Agriculture estimates that it takes $210,070 to raise a child from birth until his or her 18th birthday.

After You Listen

Talk to a classmate about your ideas: Why do you think some countries have big, extended families and some countries have small, nuclear families?

In many families in the United States and Canada, pets are part of the family. The family dog often sleeps on the bed with the children or parents. There are sometimes pictures of the family pet on the wall along with pictures of the children.

During Christmas, you can even bring your cat or dog to see Santa Claus in the shopping mall. (But not on the same day, please!) Is this true in your native culture?

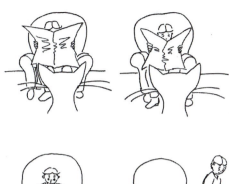

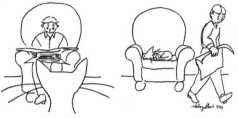

Getting Ready to Listen

You will hear people discuss their pets. What do you think they will say? Check off your predictions.

_____ The name of the pet   _____ The breed of the pet

_____ The size of the pet   _____ The personality of the pet

_____ The color of the pet   _____ The food eaten by the pet

_____ The length of hair   _____ The age of the pet
of the pet

_____ The kind of animal   _____ The habits of the pet
the pet is
(dog, cat, etc.)   _____ The special talents of the pet

Listen

Listening 2: Talking About Pets

As you listen, check off what you hear.

Part 1

_____ Her name is Emma.

_____ She's two years old.

_____ She's scared of dogs.

_____ She loves fish.

_____ She's small.

_____ She's playful.

Part 2

_____ Her name is Luce.

_____ She takes a walk every day.

_____ She's very big.

_____ She eats a lot.

_____ She loves her toys.

_____ She likes to play with other dogs.

◆ After You Listen

Do you have a pet? Introduce your pet to a small group of classmates. You might want to talk about your pet's size, color, type, personality, age, habits, and/or special talent(s).

◆ Getting Ready to Listen

You will hear some interesting facts about pets in the United States and Canada. Before you listen, read the questions in the next activity and predict the answers. Then, share your predictions with some classmates.

◆ Listen

Listening 3: Pet Statistics

Listen to check your predictions.

1. In the United States and Canada
    a. 99% of households have pets.
    b. 60% of households have pets.
    c. 30% of households have pets.

2. The most popular pets in the U.S. and Canada are
    a. dogs
    b. cats
    c. Both dogs and cats are very popular.

3. Other popular pets are
    a. birds and fish.
    b. birds and horses.
    c. birds and snakes.

4. Pets help their owners because
    a. people don't feel lonely with a pet.
    b. people with pets are healthier.
    c. Both a and b.

> A family is a unit composed not only of children but of men, women, an occasional animal, and the common cold.
>
> **—OGDEN NASH**

5. Pet owners

    a. always carry a picture of their pet.

    b. often carry a picture of their pet.

    c. sometimes carry a picture of their pet.

 **After You Listen**

Talk to a partner.

1. What did you learn about pets in the United States and Canada?

2. Did you hear anything that surprised you? What surprised you?

PART 2: Family Stories

Getting Ready to Read

You will read a story about pets who helped their owner. Have you ever heard about an animal who helped someone? Tell a classmate about it.

Vocabulary Building

Read the sentences. Try to guess the meaning of the underlined words. Then match the words with their meanings. The first one has been done for you.

1. The lake is <u>frozen</u> during the winter.

2. Thin ice can <u>break</u> if you walk on it.

3. He was afraid, and his <u>cries</u> were loud.

4. She <u>struggled</u> for many years before she was successful.

5. I stopped looking for my cat after an hour; then she suddenly <u>appeared</u>.

6. Rub your dog's <u>belly</u>! She will like it.

7. My cat <u>crawled</u> under the bed.

8. My dog wanted to chase cars, but I <u>grabbed</u> her.

9. Is that a new <u>collar</u> on your dog?

10. Pets who help people are famous for <u>heroism</u>.

_____ frozen

_____ to break

_____ a cry

__*a*__ to struggle

_____ to appear

_____ a belly

_____ to crawl

_____ to grab

_____ a collar

_____ heroism

a. to try very hard to do something, no matter how difficult

b. to suddenly be seen

c. to take hold of something quickly

d. a loud shout showing fear

e. a band put around an animal's neck

f. made very hard or turned to ice

g. very great courage or bravery

h. to move slowly with your body on or close to the ground

i. a stomach

j. to separate into two or more pieces

◆ **Read**

Brave Hearts (Brave Pets)

1   February 24, 1995, was very cold, 35 below zero. Jim Gilchrist decided to take his two dogs, Tara and Tiree, for an afternoon walk anyway. They walked through the woods. Then they headed home across a frozen lake. The dogs ran ahead. Jim felt the ice break. "I was walking along and went 'pop' right through," he remembers. "It happened so fast. I thought, 'This could be the end.'"

2   Tara heard Jim's **cries.** She ran over and fell in the water, too. As they **struggled,** Tiree **appeared.** "All I could think was that she'd meet our same fate," says Gilchrist. Instead, the dog went down to her **belly.** She **crawled** to the hole in the ice. Gilchrist **grabbed** Tiree's **collar.** Tara **climbed** on his back to jump out of the hole. Then she lay on her belly next to Tiree. Gilchrist grabbed Tara's collar with his other hand. While the 200-pound Gilchrist hung on, the dogs crawled backward until he was safe. "They could have run away," says Gilchrist. When he arrived home, he gave his dogs a hot bath. "They risked their lives to save me."

3   Tiree won several awards for **heroism.** She is a happy dog. Tara is scared of water now. So is Gilchrist. "I will never go out on the lake when it's frozen— or let my animals."

—Dan Jewel and Sopheronia Scott Gregory

After You Read

There are some expressions in this article that may be new to you. Read the sentences and circle the meaning that is closest to the underlined expressions.

1. Then they <u>headed home</u> across a frozen lake.

   a. They went in the direction of home.

   b. They pointed their heads towards home.

2. "All I could think was that she'd <u>meet our same fate</u>," says Gilchrist.

   a. To have the same experience or thing happen to you.

   b. To meet someone scary.

3. While the 200-pound Gilchrist <u>hung on</u>, the dogs crawled backward until he was safe.

   a. To call someone.

   b. To hold something tightly.

4. "They <u>risked their lives</u> to save me."

   a. To give up something.

   b. To put themselves in a very dangerous situation for something.

Getting Ready to Listen

Remember to predict before you listen. You will hear four stories about how people met their husband or wife. How do people normally meet in your native country? In other countries? Think about what you might hear. Share your predictions with classmates. Make a list here.

> Other things may change us, but we start and end with the family.
>
> —ANTHONY BRANDT

HOW PEOPLE MEET

_____

_____

_____

_____

_____

_____

Vocabulary Check

Check off the words and phrases that you know. Ask a classmate or your teacher about words and phrases you are not familiar with.

_____ senior year   _____ to date someone

_____ biology   _____ to arrange something

_____ a date   _____ a matchmaker

_____ a wedding anniversary   _____ an engineer

_____ some luggage   _____ an advertisement

 Listen

Listening 4: How People Meet

Listen to each story. How did each couple meet? Choose the answer.

1.
    a. In high school
    b. In college
    c. In graduate school

2.
    a. At a bus stop
    b. At an airport
    c. At a laundromat

3.
    a. Through their church
    b. Through their friends
    c. Through their parents

4.
    a. Through a friend
    b. Through a personal ad
    c. Through a matchmaker

 **After You Listen**

Go back to your list of predictions on p. 222. Put a check mark next to items that you heard. Which answers were surprising to you? Talk to a partner about answers that surprised you.

TUNING IN: "Looking for Love"

Discuss these questions with a partner:

1. Do you know someone who is looking for love?

2. If yes, what is this person doing to meet someone?

3. Have you ever heard of someone advertising for a mate? If yes, what do you think of this way of meeting someone?

© CNN

SWM 41 with big heart seeks **SWF** with same for LTR. Enjoys walks in the woods, travel, biking, and fine wine. Have love and time to share? Don't wait, call today.

Now watch the video. As you watch, check off the ways that people advertise for a mate.

_____ an ad on the wall of a café

_____ an ad in the newspaper

_____ a flyer given to people on the street

_____ a commercial on TV

_____ a billboard on the highway

Discuss these questions in a small group:

1. Why do you think people try this way to meet someone?

2. Is it difficult to meet a husband or wife in your native culture? Why or why not?

3. Here's an advertisement. It's for a singles club for people who like adventure and outdoor activities. What do you think? Would you join this club to meet a mate?

In the past, most North Americans got married in their early twenties. They often met their husband or wife in high school or in college. These days, many North American adults wait until they are older to get married. However, they sometimes have a difficult time meeting someone. Some people join singles clubs to meet someone special. Or they place a "personal ad" in a newspaper or magazine. Internet dating services are becoming popular ways to meet people as well.

LANGUAGE YOU CAN USE: USING TIME EXPRESSIONS TO TELL A STORY

We often use time expressions when we tell a story. Here are some useful time expressions that you may want to use when telling a story:

Expression	Example
One day, . . .	One day, we joked that we should go on a date.
That night, . . .	That night, we talked and laughed.
While . . .	While we waited for her luggage, I heard a man speaking Italian.
When . . .	When I met my wife, I knew she was the one for me.
The next day, . . .	The next day, he called me.
Then . . .	Then we started to get to know each other.
At first, . . .	At first, I was very nervous.
After a while, . . .	After a while, I started to like her.
Finally, . . .	Finally, we got married.

USING NEW LANGUAGE

Work with a partner.

1. Tell your partner how your parents met or how you met your husband/wife or boyfriend/girlfriend. Or tell about another interesting meeting you know about. Use the expressions above.

2. Listen to your partner's story. Write the time expressions you hear below:

_____

_____

_____

_____

The Sound of It: The Simple Past /-ed/ Sound

Often when you tell a story, you use the simple past. The simple past is formed by adding *-ed* to the base form of regular verbs. It is very important to *hear* the *-ed* sound in English when listening. The *-ed* ending tells you that something happened in the past. It is also very important to *pronounce* the *-ed* ending correctly so that people will understand you are talking about the past.

Listen for /-ed/ Endings

Listen to some sentences and decide if the verb is in the simple past or the simple present. Write the verb in the correct column.

SIMPLE PRESENT	SIMPLE PAST
1. _____	_____
2. _____	_____
3. _____	_____
4. _____	_____
5. _____	_____

> No matter what you've done for yourself or for humanity, if you can't look back on having given love and attention to your own family, what have you really accomplished?
>
> —LIDO ANTHONY "LEE" IACOCCA

Pronunciation of /-ed/ Endings

There are three ways to pronounce *-ed* endings in English. Listen to these sentences from the stories.

> We *talked* and *laughed* a lot during class. /t/
> I *answered* the door. /d/
> We *dated* for a year. /id/

Voiced sounds have a vibration. Unvoiced sounds do not.

> *-ed* is pronounced /t/ after unvoiced sounds like /k/ and /f/.
> *-ed* is pronounced /d/ after voiced sounds like /v/ and /z/.
> *-ed* is pronounced as an extra syllable, /id/, after verbs that end in /t/ and /d/.

Listening Practice

Listen to some sentences from the stories. Circle the pronunciation of the *-ed* ending.

1. /t/   /d/   /id/

2. /t/   /d/   /id/

3. /t/   /d/   /id/

4. /t/   /d/   /id/

5. /t/   /d/   /id/

Tell a Story

Practice using *-ed* endings in your speaking. Work with a partner. Retell the story from "Brave Hearts (Brave Pets)." Remember to pronounce the *-ed* endings clearly. Listen when your partner is talking. Can you hear the *-ed* endings clearly?

PART 3: Family Responsibilities

LANGUAGE LEARNING STRATEGY

Repeat new words and phrases several times. You will hear many new words in English every day. Sometimes it is difficult to remember all that you hear. So repeat new words and phrases several times. This will help you remember them more easily. Then use each word soon.

Apply the Strategy

Read the following list of family responsibilities. Check off the responsibilities you are familiar with. Then repeat each new phrase several times.

FAMILY RESPONSIBILITIES	
_____ make the beds	_____ wash the dishes
_____ earn money	_____ do the shopping
_____ clean the bathroom	_____ fix the sink
_____ do the yard work	_____ pay the bills
_____ plan the meals	_____ cook the dinner
_____ set the table	_____ paint the house
_____ take care of the children	_____ empty the dishwasher
_____ rake the lawn	_____ take care of the garden

(continued on next page)

Work with a partner. One partner points to a part of the house below. The other partner says something you might do there. Use the vocabulary on the previous page.

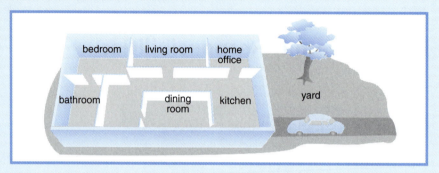

LANGUAGE YOU CAN USE:
TALKING ABOUT RESPONSIBILITIES

Here are some expressions for talking about responsibilities:

EXPRESSION	EXAMPLE
have to	I *have to* set the table before dinner.
	My sister *has to* empty the dishwasher.
need to	They *need to* rake the lawn.
	You *need to* do the yard work.
must	I *must* pay the bills today.
	We *must* wash the dishes now.

USING NEW LANGUAGE

Tell a partner about the responsibilities of each member of your family. Use the phrases above.

My mother . . .   My husband/wife . . .

My father . . .   My children . . .

My parents . . .   I . . .

My sister/brother . . .   We all . . .

Write About It.

Now write a paragraph about the responsibilities of each member of your family. Example:

> In my family, we all have different responsibilities. My mother has to pay the bills, set the table, wash the dishes, and empty the dishwasher. My father must plan the meals, do the shopping, cook the dinner, and take care of the garden. They both need to earn money. I need to rake the lawn, paint the house, and do the yard work. Together, we have to take care of the house and each other!

ACADEMIC POWER STRATEGY

Make a schedule to use your time well. Making a schedule can help you plan everything you need to do. Each week, plan your schoolwork, responsibilities, and appointments on a schedule. Don't forget to schedule time for friends and family, too. Remember to follow your schedule. When it's your time with family, don't study, and when it's your time to study, don't make phone calls or talk to friends.

Apply the Strategy

Make a schedule for the next week. Then follow your schedule and use your time well.

Weekly Schedule							
	SUN	MON	TUES	WED	THUR	FRI	SAT
6 am							
7 am							
8 am							
9 am							
10 am							
11 am							
12 pm							

(continued on next page)

Weekly Schedule							
	SUN	MON	TUES	WED	THUR	FRI	SAT
1 pm							
2 pm							
3 pm							
4 pm							
5 pm							
6 pm							
7 pm							
8 pm							
9 pm							
10 pm							
11 pm							
12 am							

PUTTING IT ALL TOGETHER

 **Presentation**

Prepare a short presentation for your classmates.

1. Choose one of these topics:

   a. Tell a story about a pet or about an animal hero.

   b. Tell a story about a family member.

   c. Tell a story about an event or experience from your life.

2. Plan to use time expressions and the simple past to tell your story.

3. Practice.

4. Tell your story to the class.

Half the class should listen for time expressions and write what they hear. The other half of the class should listen for simple past *-ed* endings and check the sounds they hear, /t/, /d/, or /id/.

Test-Taking Tip

Don't spend too much time on one question. If you have problems with a question, move on to other questions. Come back to the difficult question later. If you still don't know the answer, try to make a logical guess. Don't leave any questions unanswered.

CHECK YOUR PROGRESS

On a scale of 1 to 5, rate how well you have mastered the goals set at the beginning of the chapter:

1 2 3 4 5   ask about and give information about families.

1 2 3 4 5   predict what you will hear.

1 2 3 4 5   use time expressions to tell a story.

1 2 3 4 5   pronounce simple past *-ed* endings correctly.

1 2 3 4 5   repeat new words and phrases several times.

1 2 3 4 5   talk about responsibilities.

1 2 3 4 5   make a schedule to use your time well.

If you've given yourself a 3 or lower on any of these goals:

- visit the *Tapestry* web site for additional practice.

- ask your instructor for extra help.

- review the sections of the chapter that you found difficult.

- work with a partner or study group to further your progress.

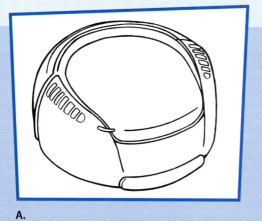

A.

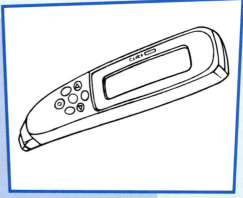

B.

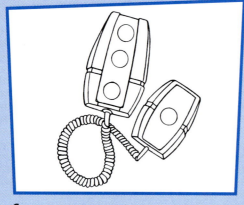

C.

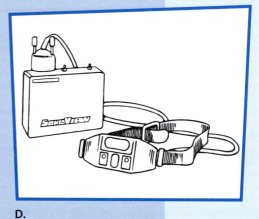

D.

Look at these pictures of new inventions that will help us in the future. Discuss these questions with your classmates:

- What do you think each invention does?
- Do you think these inventions will be useful? Why or why not?
- What other kinds of inventions do you think will exist in the future?

10

THE FUTURE IS NOW

People like to think about the future. They like to imagine the answers to questions like these: What new inventions will improve the way we live? How will we move from place to place? Will we use cars? How will those cars run? Where will we live? What will our houses be like? What will our jobs be like? This chapter is about life in the future. You will learn about new inventions that could be part of our lives in the future. You will also make some guesses about what you think life will be like in the future.

Setting Goals

In this chapter you will:

◆ retell what you hear to someone else.

◆ make predictions about the future.

◆ use pictures and photos to help identify main ideas.

◆ talk about plans for the future.

◆ use question intonation to change statements into questions.

◆ change the tone of your voice when asking different kinds of questions.

◆ reward yourself for reaching goals.

233

◆ Getting Started

> **I don't try to describe the future; I try to prevent it.**
>
> —RAY BRADBURY

1. Match the photo in the introduction with the description of each invention.

   _____ A vacuum cleaner that will vacuum your house automatically.

   _____ A pen that will scan a book and translate the words into other languages.

   _____ A machine that will help you park your car without hitting something.

   _____ A sensor that will help blind people to see.

2. With a partner, look all the photos and pictures in this chapter. Describe what you see in each photo and picture. Think about the title of this chapter: "The Future Is Now." Discuss how you think the pictures and photos are connected to the future.

Culture Note

People in the United States like to think about the future. They like to watch movies about what life will be like in the future. These kinds of movies are called science fiction movies. Have you seen any of these science fiction movies—*Star Trek, Star Wars, Jurassic Park, Waterworld,* or *Mad Max?*

PART 1: Gadgets and Games

Gadgets are mechanical devices. This part of the chapter tells about mechanical devices and games that will make our lives more interesting in the future.

LANGUAGE LEARNING STRATEGY

Repeat or retell what you hear to someone else in order to make sure you understand what you have heard. When what you are listening to is long, you can make notes or fill in a graphic organizer. Then you can look at your notes as you retell what you heard.

Apply the Strategy

Work with a partner. Complete this listening activity. When you finish, retell what you hear to your partner. You may use a graphic organizer to help you.

Getting Ready to Listen

Look at these photos of toys and games. They are different from traditional toys and games because of their use of technology. How do you think modern toys are different from more traditional toys? Are they more or less interesting? Are they more or less fun to play with? Are they more or less educational?

Listen

Listening 1: Toys of the Future

Look at the picture of each toy as you listen to the tape. Then listen again. Fill in the semantic map as you listen.

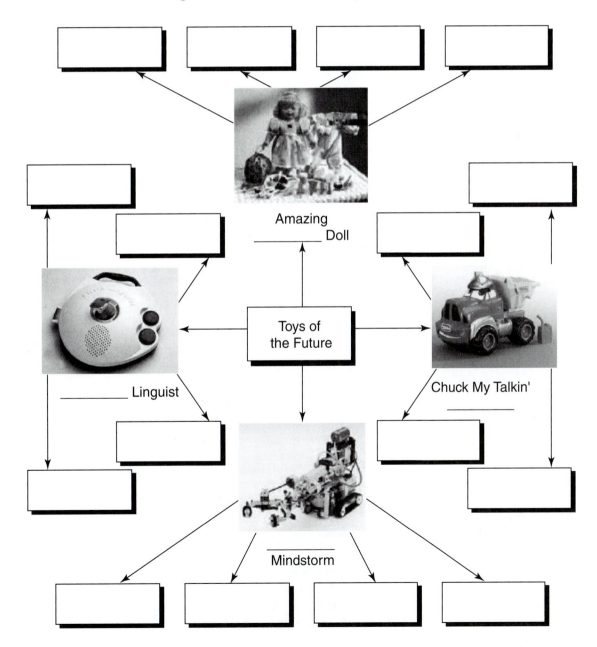

Amazing _____ Doll

_____ Linguist

Toys of the Future

Chuck My Talkin' _____

Mindstorm

The United States is a country that likes its toys. Each year people in the United States spend 70 billion dollars on toys, games, and sports equipment. There are many advertisements for toys on television, especially during the winter holiday season. There is controversy about the idea that there is too much pressure put on parents to buy expensive toys for their children during this season. People say that many parents can't afford these toys and that the focus on toys and gifts takes away from the enjoyment of the holiday season. Is there a similar focus on toys and gifts during holidays in your native country?

 **After You Listen**

Now work with a partner. Take turns retelling what you heard about the different toys in the listening activity. Use your graphic organizer to help you retell what you heard. When it is your turn to listen, make sure to listen to your partner carefully. Remind your partner of anything he or she missed when retelling about the toys.

Small Group Discussion

Which of these toys will be successful in the future? Explain why you think it will be successful.

LANGUAGE YOU CAN USE: FUTURE PREDICTIONS

Use *will* to make predictions about the future. There are two ways to make the negative with *will: will not* and *won't. Will* and *will not* are more formal. We usually use the contractions *'ll* and *won't* when speaking. Look at these examples:

I will drive an electric car in the future.

The car will not pollute the air.

We'll go to work four days a week.

You won't have to work so hard.

Children won't be bored.

They'll interact with toys.

USING NEW LANGUAGE

What do you predict life will be like twenty years from now? Work with a partner. Take a few minutes to think about each of these questions. Tell your partner your prediction. Explain your prediction. See the example on the next page.

The earliest computers used to fill entire rooms. Today, lap-top computers are small enough to take with you in a bag wherever you want to go. Eventually, computers will be small enough to wear. The "computer-band" will be worn on your arm, have a built-in telephone, and allow you to connect to the Internet from anywhere. It will be powered by a special vest that is worn by the user. This vest will convert body heat into electricity.

—CONCEPT FROM *FUTURE* BY MICHAEL TAMBINI

In the future, digital televisions could be a TV, computer, and telephone all in one. Then you would need only one system for entertainment, communication, research, and shopping at home.

Example: Most cars will run on electricity twenty years from now, because gasoline will be very expensive.

1. What will cars run on?
2. What will houses be like?
3. What kind of job will you have?
4. How will computers help people?
5. Will there be homeless people?
6. What will schools be like?
7. What diseases will doctors cure?
8. Will we discover life on other planets?
9. Will people live longer?
10. What will fashion be like?

Small Group Discussion

Before you look at the video "Smart House," discuss these questions with two or three other students. In the beginning of this chapter, there is a photograph of a vacuum that cleans by itself. What other inventions do you think might be in houses in the future? What inventions will make our lives easier? What inventions will make our houses safer?

TUNING IN: "Smart House"

This video is about a house of the future. It's called the Smart House. The Smart House uses computers and electronics to save energy and make life easier, safer, and more comfortable. Watch the video. Fill in the semantic map on the next page as you listen. Listen to the video again to make sure the information is correct. Then retell the information you heard to your partner.

© CNN

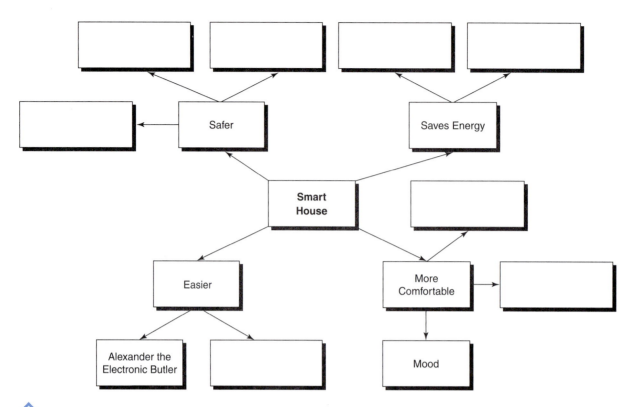

◆ Think About It

Without electricity, the "smart house" becomes a "dumb house." Do you think modern inventions make the quality of our lives better, or do they just add more stress to our lives when they do not work right?

◆ Talk About It

What inventions will make our life easier in the future? Work with a group of four students. Think of an invention that would make life easier in the future. (For example, you might invent a car that repairs itself when it breaks down, or you could invent an international translator that fits into your ear like a hearing aid. When you wear it, you will be able to understand what any person is saying in any language.) Then do this:

1. Organize your group. Choose roles for each group member.

Roles

Facilitator: makes sure that all group members participate.

Illustrator: takes the group's ideas and makes pictures of them.

Recorder: writes down the ideas.

Presenter: organizes the recorder's notes and makes a presentation to the whole class.

Experts say that by the year 2020, all telephones will be video phones. Improved technology will allow more digital information to be sent over the airwaves. In addition to seeing who you are talking to face to face, you'll be able to send photographs and printed words over the telephone.

—CONCEPT FROM *FUTURE* BY MICHAEL TAMBINI

2. Create an invention.

- With your group, make a drawing of the invention.

- Decide at least three things the invention will be able to do.

- Decide how it will make people's lives easier.

- Hang the pictures of the inventions around the room.

3. Explain the invention.

- Your teacher will send you to meet with a person in another group.

- Share your group's invention. Listen to the other person as she or he tells about her or his group's invention.

- Ask him or her questions about the invention.

4. Retell what you learned.

- Go back to your original group. Retell what you learned about other groups' inventions.

Class Discussion

Look at the pictures of all of the inventions. Decide which will be the most useful. Which is the most creative? Which is the most realistic?

Talk About It

Look at the topics below and choose one that you think you could tell a story about. Tell your partner a short story about the topic you have chosen. It can be a true or imagined story. Stop before the end of the story. Your partner will predict the end. When it is your turn to predict the end of your partner's story, listen to him or her carefully.

TOPICS

A Terrible Vacation

A Famous Person I Met

A Time I Was Really Afraid

The Best Party

Something That Was Hard to Learn

EXAMPLE:

When I was young, I wanted to play the guitar. I wanted to be a rock musician. I told my parents that I would like guitar lessons. For Christmas, they gave me a guitar. I started taking guitar lessons. I found out that the guitar is not an easy instrument. Each hand is doing something different. For one month I practiced the guitar every day. Guess what happened?

PART 2: Electric Wheels

Do you remember the video from Chapter 2 about the electric car, the Sparrow? What do you remember about that video? This section has more information about electric cars.

Vocabulary Building

There are clues in the passage that tell you words have similar meanings. Guess what words below have similar meanings. As you read, look for these words. Check to see if your guesses are correct.

1. sick	_____ distance
2. recharged	_____ bi-fuel
3. motor	_____ ill
4. two different kinds of fuel	_____ a few
5. a little	_____ fuel
6. limited range	_____ used again
7. gas	_____ engine

Getting Ready to Read

This reading passage has information about electric cars. Before you read this passage, read the title and the subtitles. Make a list of three things you might read about in this passage, but do not copy the subtitles exactly.

1. _____

2. _____

3. _____

This reading passage is another way to practice predicting what words will come next. There are some words missing in this passage. However, you can see the first letter of the missing word. Read the passage one time. Then read the passage again and work with a partner to try to guess the missing words. Your teacher will help you check your answers.

Culture Note

Americans love their cars, and they drive a lot. The average licensed driver in the United States drives more than 13,000 miles each year.

Read

Electric Cars

Electric Cars Fight Pollution

Some people believe that electric cars will be the cars of the future. Other people are not ready to give up their gas-powered cars so soon. Why have electric cars? Electric cars are really cool looking. They are quieter than gas-powered cars. However, the most important reason people will have electric cars in the future is to reduce air pollution. In big cities like Los Angeles, cars can cause most of the air pollution. Pollution in big cities causes lung problems. People are getting sick. If pollution is not reduced, more people will get ill.

How Electric Cars Work

The basic mechanics of electric cars are simple. T_____ are just cars with electric motors. They have e_____ batteries instead of a gas tank. The major a_____ of electric cars is that they can be recharged a_____ an electric outlet. They don't make pollution, and they u_____ no gasoline.

Problems with Electric Cars

The technology for electric cars is getting b_____. At first, electric cars did not go v_____ fast. Now some electric cars can drive 75 m_____ per hour or more. There are still some p_____ with electric cars. Most electric cars have limited range. They c_____ go only a short distance before they n_____ to be recharged. However, most can g_____ about 60 miles on one charge. The f_____ of electric cars looks bright. Scientists will m_____ improvements to these batteries. Another problem is that electric c_____ are more expensive than gasoline-powered vehicles. M_____ people think the price of electric cars w_____ go down in the future.

Some people believe t_____ electric cars will not be common in t_____ future. They say plants that produce electricity a_____ cause pollution. However, electric power plants are m_____ efficient than gas-powered engines. Electric power p_____ do not pollute as much as individual g_____ motors in each car. Also, some kinds of electric p_____, such as solar and wind, do not make a_____ pollution at all.

Bi-fuel cars
·············

Carmakers are also looking at o_____ ways of reducing air pollution from cars. S_____ cars and trucks will run on natural gas. O_____ cars are bi-fueled. This means they use two different kinds of fuel. For example, one kind o_____ car will use both gasoline and electricity. T_____ car starts using gasoline and then runs o_____ electricity on the highway. It can run f_____ a long time on only a few gallons of gas.

> About 86% of the workers in the United States commute to work by car. Five percent use public transportation. Four percent walk to work. The rest work at home or go to work by motorcycle, bicycle, or other means.

◆ **After You Read**

When you finish the reading passage, compare your answers with other students in the class. Then check your answers with your teacher. Did you make good predictions? If the words you guessed were not exactly correct, did they make sense?

LANGUAGE LEARNING STRATEGY

U se pictures and photos to help you guess the main idea before you listen. Before you listen, look at photos, pictures, and graphs that go with the listening passage. The visuals can help you guess the main idea of the passage. This will help you understand the passage better.

Apply the Strategy

Before you listen, look at the picture and predict what the listening passage will be about.

Listen to the tape. Look at the two possible endings for the passage. Predict which is the correct ending to the passage. Then start the tape again and check your answer.

1. a. It can carry only two passengers.

   b. It can carry no passengers.

   c. It can carry five passengers.

2. a. It can go 25 miles per hour.

   b. It can go 150 miles per hour.

   c. It can go 65 miles per hour.

3. a. It is not for sale yet, but you won't want to buy it.

   b. It is not for sale yet, but it will be available soon.

   c. It is not for sale yet, because it cannot be recharged.

◇ Practice Outside of Class

Predicting what a speaker says is a good way to improve your listening skills. You can practice this skill when you watch TV or a movie in English. Try this. The next time you watch TV or a movie in English, cover your ears for a few seconds and guess what the person is talking about by looking at the person's body language or facial expression. Uncover your ears and check to see if your prediction is correct. (However, remember it is not polite to cover your ears when you are listening to a real person!)

◀ Talk About It

In the future, a device called Smart Garbage Can will help keep your kitchen clean. The Smart Garbage Can will sort and crush your garbage into compact bundles that can be easily collected and recycled. The Smart Garbage Can will also come with special filters that will help keep your garbage from smelling.

—CONCEPT FROM *FUTURE* BY MICHAEL TAMBINI

Air pollution is a big problem all over the world today. Now you know some information about electric cars. They might reduce pollution in the future. However, there are other ways of reducing pollution. Here is your chance to give your opinion about electric cars and ways to reduce air pollution. With three or four other students, talk about the following questions. One person in your group should act as a recorder and record the answers of the other group members. Another student should act as facilitator and make sure that all students get a chance to talk.

1. Do you own a car now?

2. How many miles a day do you drive or ride?

3. What are the disadvantages of an electric car?

4. What are the advantages of an electric car?

5. Do you think you will ever drive an electric car?

6. Besides electric cars, what are some other ways to reduce air pollution?

7. How can you personally help reduce air pollution?

Now report your ideas for reducing air pollution to the whole class. Put all of the groups' ideas together in a list.

PART 3: What's Your Plan?

Making plans is an important part of preparing for the future.

LANGUAGE YOU CAN USE: TALKING ABOUT PLANS

Here are two ways to talk about plans in English: *will* and *be + going to*. When you use the *going to* form, make sure the *be* verb agrees with the subject. Look at these examples:

I'm (I am) going to have a birthday party for my sister.

You're (You are) going to bake the cake for the party.

Joseph's (Joseph is) going to buy the ice cream.

My mom's (mom is) going to invite all of her friends.

We're (We are) going to have a surprise party.

She's (she is) going to be surprised.

They're (They are) going to arrive before she gets home.

Study these two sentences. Both talk about making a plan, but they each have a different meaning.

Be + going to is used to express plans that the speaker is more certain about. For example, you would say "I'm going to eat dinner after this TV program."

Will is used to express plans that the speaker is less certain about. For example, "At the end of this semester, I'll take a vacation."

USING NEW LANGUAGE

Work with a partner. Tell your partner your plan by finishing each of these sentences. Decide if each requires distant or immediate plans.

EXAMPLE: After class today, I'm going to do my homework.

1. After class today,

2. When I graduate from college,

3. Before the next test in this class,

4. When I get home today,

5. When the semester is over,

6. Next summer,

7. Before dinner,

8. During vacation,

9. The next time I travel,

10. When I wake up tomorrow,

11. Sometime in the future,

The Sound of It: Question Intonation

Usually when we ask a question in English, we change the order of the words. Compare these sentences:

What are you going to do in the future?

I am going to graduate next week.

What will be on the test?

There will be questions about the future tense on the test.

However, you can change a statement into a question just by changing the intonation of your voice. If the tone of your voice goes up at the end of a statement, it means you are not sure about the statement and are asking a question. Listen to your teacher say this statement with question intonation. Listen again as he or she says the same statement without question intonation:

You're going to eat that?

You're going to eat that.

Try It Out

Work with a partner. Practice saying these statements with and without question intonation. Can you hear the difference?

You'll finish by Saturday.	You'll finish by Saturday?
I'm going to see you there.	I'm going to see you there?
She's going to have a party.	She's going to have a party?
We're going to make plans.	We're going to make plans?
They'll be here by six.	They'll be here by six?
It's going to be crowded.	It's going to be crowded?

Intonation and Different Kinds of Questions

Listen carefully as your teacher asks these questions:

What are you going to do after class?

Are you going to study after class?

Does his or her voice sound different at the end of each question? When you ask an information question (a question that begins with *who, what, when, where,* or *how*), the tone of your voice usually rises a little at the end of the question. When you ask a yes/no question, the tone of your voice goes down at the end of a question. Listen to your teacher say the two questions again. Now can you hear the difference in his or her voice? Work with a partner. Practice asking and answering the following questions. Pay attention to the rising or falling tone of voice at the end of each question.

1. Where are you going to go after class today?
2. Will you graduate from college next year?
3. When are you going to study for the next test?
4. Is he going to eat when he gets home?
5. What will you do when the semester is over?
6. Will they take a vacation next summer?
7. Who is going to be there before dinner?
8. Will you see your family during vacation?
9. Will you take a train the next time you travel?
10. What time are you going to wake up tomorrow?

Making Plans

Work with a group of students. Imagine that your group has been asked to plan an event. Possible events include a fund raiser for a homeless shelter, a trip to a children's hospital or retirement community, a campus or city beautification event, or an international day on your campus. You need to decide things like these:

- What kind of event are you planning?
- How will you get people to come to your event?
- Who will you ask?
- Will you serve food?
- Where will the event be held?
- What special materials will you need?
- Who will do each task?

After you make plans for the event, tell the other students in the group about your event and the plans you made for the event.

ACADEMIC POWER STRATEGY

Reward yourself for reaching your goals. Short-term goals are goals that you set for the near future. You can create your own short-term goals. For example, if your goal is to learn irregular past tense verbs, you can break your goal down into several short-term goals. Your short-term goal may be to study ten new verbs every day for five days. One way to encourage yourself to reach the goals you plan is to reward yourself for accomplishing those goals.

Apply the Strategy

Think about each of the areas on the following chart. Write a long-term goal for each area. Write some short-term goals that will help you accomplish your long-term goals. Then plan some rewards for when you reach your goals. For example, if your academic goal is to get a higher score on your next test, you would write this: "to get a higher grade on my next grammar test." Then you might write: "I'm going to study 30 minutes every day for 5 days before the test." Other short-term goals could include asking your teacher a question about something you don't understand or studying with another student a little bit every day. You will probably have several short-term goals to help you accomplish your long-term goal.

Now think about things you like, things you would consider as a way to reward yourself. Write these ideas in the last column of the chart. For example, if you like ice cream, you may reward yourself by eating some ice cream after you finish studying each day. Or if you like video games, you could reward yourself with 15 minutes of video games after you study.

Long-Term Goal	Short-Term Goals	Possible Rewards
Academic Goal		
Career Goal		
Language Learning Goal		

PUTTING IT ALL TOGETHER

Your teacher may assign one or all of the activities below:

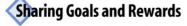 **Sharing Goals and Rewards**

1. Form a group of three people.

2. The first group member tells about a goal he or she has and a reward he or she plans to give himself or herself when the goal has been accomplished.

3. The second group member asks three questions about the first member's goal or reward.

4. The third group member retells what the first two members said.

5. Repeat this process until all three members have described a reward.

Body Parts

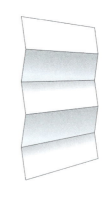

1. Work with a group of five students.

2. Sit in a circle.

3. Each student needs a blank piece of paper. Fold the paper into five equal parts. Then unfold the paper. Your paper should look like this:

4. In the top section of the paper, draw a head. You can continue the lines for the neck a little past the fold. Then fold the part with the head back like this:

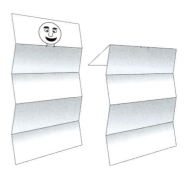

5. Pass the paper on to the person at your right. This person should not look at what the last person drew. On the next section of paper, this person should draw the neck, shoulders, and arms. This person should fold the drawing back, then pass the paper to his or her right.

6. Continue like this. The third person will draw the trunk of a body, the fourth will draw legs, and the last one will draw feet.

7. Open the paper. Show the drawings to all members of the group. With your group members, make up a name for each "character" (drawing).

8. Then make up a story about what will happen when these characters meet one day in the future. Share your story with the other groups.

Interview a Speaker

Invite a native English speaker to your class. Work with your classmates. Plan some questions you would like to ask the speaker. Here are some possible speakers and topics:

- Ask an administrator or school official about the plans for your school in the future.

- Ask a city official about his or her plans for your city in the future.

- Ask the director of your English program how your program might change in the future.

- Ask a career counselor how different jobs might change in the future.

- Ask a doctor what diseases may be cured in the future.

Be sure to thank the person you invite to your class.

Write About It.

Do you think life will be better or worse in the future? Give examples of ways life will be better or worse. After you write, share your opinions with your classmates.

Test-Taking Tip

Don't panic when students start handing in their papers. Don't let other students leaving distract or rush you. No one gets extra points for finishing a test early. In fact, students who take all the test time available to them are likely to hand in more careful, well-thought-out tests.

CHECK YOUR PROGRESS

On a scale of 1 to 5, rate how well you have mastered the goals set at the beginning of the chapter:

1 2 3 4 5   retell what you hear to someone else.

1 2 3 4 5   make predictions about the future.

1 2 3 4 5   use pictures and photos to help identify main ideas.

1 2 3 4 5   talk about plans for the future.

1 2 3 4 5   use question intonation to change statements into questions.

1 2 3 4 5   change the tone of your voice when asking different kinds of questions.

1 2 3 4 5   reward yourself for reaching goals.

If you've given yourself a 3 or lower on any of these goals:

- visit the *Tapestry* web site for additional practice.

- ask your instructor for extra help.

- review the sections of the chapter that you found difficult.

- work with a partner or study group to further your progress.

TRANSCRIPTS

CHAPTER 1: MEETINGS AND GREETINGS

Listening 1, page 4:
Formal and Informal Introductions

Kenji: This is my friend Susan.
Sam: Hi, Susan. I'm Sam.
Susan: Hi, Sam.

Young: I'd like you to meet my teacher, Mr. Page.
Adele: It's nice to meet you.
Mr. Page: It's nice to meet you, too.

John Walker: Hello, I'm John Walker.
Anuschka Neuwald: It's good to meet you, Mr. Walker. I'm Anuschka Neuwald.

Guy: Hi, I'm Guy. Are you a new student too?
Paula: Yeah, I'm Paula.

Jorge: I don't think we've met. I'm Jorge Silva.
Mr. McCabe: It's a pleasure to meet you, Jorge. I'm Mr. McCabe. I'll be your counselor.

Listening 2, page 6:
Formal and Informal Dialogues

At a Party
Mark: Hey, George! This is Sal, my brother.
George: It is certainly a pleasure to meet you, Sal.
Sal: Nice to meet you.

In the Classroom
Mr. Macy: I'm Mr. John Macy, your grammar teacher.
Mike: Yo, what's up, Teach?

In the Cafeteria
Stephanie: Hello, Victor. I'd like you to meet a new classmate. This is Karen.
Victor: Hey, Karen. Nice to meet you.
Karen: Nice to meet you.

At Home
Paul: Patrick, this is my mother, Mrs. Doris Bluefield.
Patrick: Hey, Doris. How's it goin'?
Mrs. Bluefield: Welcome to our home, Patrick.

Listening 3, page 13:
Listen for Rate of Speech

In a Museum

Roy: Good evening, Dr. Jensen.
Dr. Jensen: Good evening, Roy. Are you here to see the new exhibit?
Roy: Yes, I am. I'm looking forward to seeing it.

In a Supermarket

Mr. Frank: Hello, Estella. How are you doing?
Estella: Oh, hello, Mr. Frank. I'm great. How are you?
Mr. Frank: Just fine, thanks.

In the Student Union

Jeff: Hey, Lester! What's happening?
Lester: Jeff! Long time no see. What's up?
Jeff: Not much.

At a Holiday Dinner

June: Hi, Aunt Elena. Oh, you look great!
Aunt Elena: Thanks. You don't look too bad yourself. Come here and give me a hug!

At the Front Door

Mr. Escobar: Good morning, Ms. Marcel. Here's your mail.
Ms. Marcel: Good morning, Mr. Escobar. Thank you so much.

In a Professor's Office

Professor Iacco: Hello, Carmen.
Carmen: Good afternoon, Professor Iacco.

Professor Iacco: Can I help you?

Carmen: Yes. I'm having some trouble with the homework.

The Sound of It, page 14: Reductions

1. How are you doing?   /How ya doin'?/

2. How is it going?   /How'zit goin'?/

3. What is happening?   /What's happ'nin'?/

4. How are you?   /How'r ya?/

5. How have you been?   /How'v ya been?/

6. It's nice to see you.   /It's nice ta see ya./

7. How about you?   /How 'bout you?/

CHAPTER 2: FINDING YOUR WAY

Listening 1, page 32:
Following Directions

Directions from San Francisco to
West Valley Community College

Hello and thank you for calling West Valley Community College. For information about classes, press 1 now. For directions to West Valley College, press 2 now. To speak to the campus operator, press 3 now. Or, if you are calling from a rotary telephone, stay on the line and the operator will assist you.

Directions to West Valley Community College. For directions from the San Jose area, press 1 now. For directions from Oakland, press 2 now. For directions from the San Francisco area, press 3 now.

Directions to West Valley Community College from San Francisco. From San Francisco, take highway 101 south. Continue south for approximately 20 miles. Then take highway 85 south. Go south on 85 for about 7 miles. Take the Saratoga Ave. exit west. Continue on Saratoga Ave. for 2 blocks. Turn left at the first traffic signal onto Fruitvale Ave. Make another left on Allendale Ave. past the church. Take the second right into the campus parking lot.

Listening 2, page 38:
Asking for Directions

New Student: Excuse me? Can you tell me how to get to Language Arts building?

Student: Sure. *Follow* Campus Center Walk *past* the Campus Center. Then *bear right* onto the bridge.

New Student: I'm sorry. Bear right?

Student: *Walk* a little to the *right* but don't *turn right* all the way. *Take* a *left* after the bridge. The Language Arts building is the *first* building on the *right*. It's *across from* the Physical Education building.

New Student: OK. So I *take* Campus Center Walk *past* the Campus Center. I *bear right* onto the bridge. I *turn left* after the bridge, and it's the *first* building on the *right*.

Student: You got it!

New Student: Thanks a lot.

Student: No problem.

Listening Activity, page 41:
Where Is the Destination?

1. Now, let's see. We're near Parking Lot 4. Walk up North Walk. Go past the Science Math building. Keep walking until you go over the bridge. Then bear right. It's the first building on the right, across from the Art Studios.

2. Oh, sure. That building is close to Parking Lot 7. Start at West College Circle. Take North Walk past a bunch of buildings until you cross the bridge. After the bridge, walk past one more building. The building you want is the second on the left, next to the Music building.

3. OK. From the Campus Center, take Campus Center Walk towards the Language Arts building. Across from the Language Arts building is the Physical Education building. The building you want is behind the PE building, next to the pool.

Listening Activity, page 47:
Listen for Syllables

Listen to these words. How many syllables are there? Write the number of syllables next to each word.

_____ television   _____ class

_____ campus   _____ library

_____ studio   _____ study

Listening Activity, page 47:
Listen for Syllable Stress

(Beep beep! Honk! Honk! Screeching car sounds)

Angry man: Hey, buddy! Get outta my way!

Angry woman: Hey, look where you're goin'!

Announcer: Does this sound all too familiar? Are you one of the *millions* of Americans who spends too much time in your car *commuting*? Well, the *Community* Transportation Service is here to help you. We have *information* about a variety of *transportation* alternatives. What about taking the *train*? Riding the bus? Using your *bike* or your feet? We can give you *public* transportation information or help you find *people* to share the ride in your *automobile*.

    Call now and let us help you escape from your car. It's free, and it could change your life! Call (650) COMMUTE. That's (650) 266-6883. Call now!

CHAPTER 3: A FULL LIFE

Listening Activity, page 54:
Vocabulary Building

1.
    A: How was your day?
    B: Oh, nothing special. It was a *typical* day.

2.
    A: Do you live off campus?
    B: No. I live in a *dorm room* here on campus. It's very convenient.

3.
    A: Do you enjoy having a *roommate?*
    B: Yeah. It's my first experience sharing a room, but it's really nice to have someone to talk to.

4.
    A: Do you need help choosing a major? Come to the *academic* counseling center. We can help you with school decisions.
    B: Thanks. I think I'll come!

5.
    A: Teenagers in the United States are so *independent.*
    B: It's true. They often move out of their parents' house when they go to college.

6.
    A: When I was a college student, all the students were young.

7.
    B: Yeah, I remember that, too. But these days, the student population is more *multigenerational.*

7.
    A: Did you go to the *multicultural* fair today?
    B: Yeah. It was really interesting. I tried some Korean BBQ, had some Thai iced tea, and watched a Native American dance.

8.
    A: Did your mother have a professional *career,* or did she work at home?
    B: Actually, she did both. When we were young, she stayed home. Later, she went back to school and became a lawyer.

9.
    A: Do you use the *Internet?*
    B: Yes! I got a new computer for Christmas. Now I surf the net every night!

10.
    A: Have you ever taken a *distance learning* course?
    B: Yes, just this past semester. I took a business class. Half the class met on this campus in a classroom while the professor and the other students were in a classroom across the country.

Listening 1, page 60:
Talking About Schedules

Khaled: Hey, Marina! How's it going?

Marina: Great. It's nice to see you, Khaled. How's your semester going?

Khaled: Oh, fine. But it's so busy.

Marina: How many classes are you taking?

Khaled: I'm taking four classes, but I'm also working in the morning.

Marina: That's great! Are you working here on campus?

Khaled: Yeah. In the Student Union cafeteria. I work there Monday through Friday starting at six.

Marina: You sound busy. Do you have time to get together and have coffee?

Khaled: I'd love to. What's your schedule?

Marina: I'm on campus Tuesday and Thursday afternoons. What time do you get off work?

Khaled: I finish work at noon, but then I have class.

Marina: Oh. What about Friday? I sometimes come to use the library. Do you have class in the afternoon on Friday?

Khaled: No. Do you want to get together then?

Marina: Sounds great. We can celebrate the end of the week!

Khaled: OK. So let's meet Friday at noon in the Student Union.

Marina: See you there!

Listening 2, page 64:
Morning Person or Night Owl?

Alex: Manuel, you're not going home now, are you?

Manuel: Sorry! I have to get up early in the morning.

Alex: But it's only eleven o'clock!

Manuel: I'm usually asleep by eleven!

Alex: Not me. I always stay up late. I often work late at night.

Manuel: You must be a real night owl. I guess I'm a morning person.

Alex: A morning person?

Manuel: Yeah. I always get up early in the morning. I usually study for a few hours in the morning.

Alex: Oh. I never study in the morning. My brain doesn't work that early!

Manuel: And I never study at night!

Listening Activity, page 68:
Sentence Stress Practice

Mio: Do you like to play sports?

Lissy: Yes. I often play sports on the weekend.

Mio: What kind of sports do you play?

Lissy: I play soccer with friends on Saturdays. On Sundays I sometimes go on hikes in the mountains.

Listening 3, page 69:
An Automated Phone Service

Hello and welcome to Moviefone. If you know the name of the movie you want to see, press one. To choose from a list of current movies, press two.

The following is a list of current movies. For *Star Wars*, press one. For *ET*, press two. For *Titanic*, press three. For *Jurassic Park*, press four. For *City of Angels*, press five.

You have selected *Titanic*. To find out the theaters in your area that have *Titanic*, press one. To hear a list of theaters showing *Titanic*, press two.

You will hear a list of theaters showing *Titanic*. To select AMC Kabuki 8, press one. To select Century 16 in Mountain View, press two. To select the Park Theater, press three. To select Century 12 in Redwood City, press four.

To find out show times for *Titanic* at Century 12 in Redwood City, press one. To buy tickets, press two.

The following is a list of show times for *Titanic* at Century 12 in Redwood City: ten o'clock, one twenty, four forty, eight o'clock, and eleven twenty.

Listening 4, page 72:
Listen for the Topic

Conversation One
(at a bus stop)

A: It looks like rain.

B: I know! And it's so cold today, too.

A: Do you think it might snow?

B: I hope so! That would be fun.

A: Yeah.

Conversation Two
(at a party)

A: So what do you do?

B: I'm a technical writer. What about you?

A: I'm a physical therapist.

B: Oh really? Do you work in a hospital?

A: Actually, I work for a private practice here in town. What about you? Where do you work?

B: I work at Apple Computer. I write technical manuals.

A: How interesting.

Conversation Three
(in a café)

A: Are you a student?

B: Yes, I'm working on a paper for my class.

A: What's your paper about?

B: It's an essay about my grandparents. What about you? Are you a student, too?

A: No, I'm a teacher. I teach English at the high school.

B: Really? Maybe you could help me. I have a question.

Conversation Four
(in line at a movie theater)

A: Are you going to see *City of Angels*?

B: No, actually I already saw it. I'm going to see *Saving Private Ryan*.

A: Oh, that's a great movie. What did you think about *City of Angels*?

B: I loved it. It's very romantic.

A: Great. Thanks for the advice.

B: No problem. Enjoy the movie.

A: I will. You, too.

CHAPTER 4: IT'S RAINING CATS AND DOGS

Listening 1, page 80:
Talking About the Weather

1. How's the weather today? It's great; it's warm and sunny outside. There is a little breeze, so it's not too hot. Great! Let's go to the beach.

2. Did you enjoy visiting your family? Yes, I did, but the weather was terrible! It was cold and wet. There was snow and sleet almost every day. We had to stay inside. That's too bad, but it's not unusual. The weather is usually cold in New York this time of year.

3. Did you live here during the hurricane? Yes, I did. What a night! It was so windy that my avocado tree was blown down. It rained three inches in one hour. There was thunder and lightning all night. We were really frightened. Luckily, we were all safe, and there was no damage to our house.

4. Be careful on your way to work today. It's very foggy out there. Visibility is very low. However, we expect the fog to burn off later in the morning; then it should be a nice, sunny day.

The Sound of It, page 83:
The /ng/ Sound

ping	pin
raining	rain
bang	ban
sung	sun
long	lawn
tongue	ton
sing	sin

Listening 2, page 84:
A Weather Report

Well, it's looking a lot like spring around the nation's capital and Eastern Ontario. The weather warmed up over the weekend. Let's take a look at the temperatures. The low yesterday was 15 degrees Celsius warming up to 25 degrees during the day.

Today, look for more of the same beautiful weather. The low tonight will be about 17 and the high temperature tomorrow warming to a nice 27. The skies will be clear in the morning, but the clouds may roll in by late afternoon. There is a possibility of light showers, but I expect it to stay warm and dry.

Looking at the rest of Canada, we see that it is clear throughout the plains with clouds hanging around the east and west coasts.

Quebec looks clear, and it will be a beautiful day in both Montreal and Toronto.

If you are traveling to Vancouver, you should expect more than just a little shower.

Heavy rain is expected on the West Coast of British Columbia over night and continuing on until the morning. Those clouds will be moving this way. It might rain here on the weekend.

If you're heading east to Nova Scotia, expect cloudy weather with just occasional rain showers.

CHAPTER 5: TO YOUR HEALTH

Listening 1, page 112:
Talking About Symptoms

Conversation One
Miyoko: Hi, Wendy!
Wendy: Hello.
Miyoko: What's wrong? Are you sick?
Wendy: Yeah. I have a really bad headache.
Miyoko: Oh. I'm sorry. You want some aspirin?
Wendy: No thanks. I'm just gonna go to bed and rest.

Conversation Two
Lisa: Hey girl. What's up?
Leslie: Not much. What about you?
Lisa: Nuthin' special. Hey, are you okay?
Leslie: Yeah. I guess I'm just really sore from going to the climbing gym yesterday.
Lisa: Me, too! I guess we overdid it. My back is sore, and I have a stiff neck.
Leslie: Next time, we'd better stretch after we exercise!
Lisa: Yes! Good idea.

Conversation Three
Professor Chavez: Hi, Tony. How are you?
Tony: Not so good, Professor Chavez. I think I'm coming down with a bad cold.
Professor Chavez: Really? What's wrong?
Tony: Well, I have a stuffy nose and a cough.
Professor Chavez: Do you have a fever? You look a little warm.

Tony: Maybe. I feel kinda hot.
Professor Chavez: Tony, you should go home and go to bed. You might have the flu that's been going around.
Tony: OK. That sounds like a good idea.
Professor Chavez: Remember to drink lots of juice and get lots of rest. I hope you feel better soon!

Conversation Four
(ringing of telephone)
Stephanie: Hello?
Mom: Stephanie, it's Mom.
Stephanie: Hi, Mom.
Mom: I just called to see how you were feeling.
Stephanie: Thanks, Mom. Actually, I still have a fever.
Mom: Did you take some medicine?
Stephanie: Yeah. It's helping.
Mom: What about your stomach? Is it still bothering you?
Stephanie: Yeah. I still feel sick to my stomach.
Mom: Oh honey, I'm sorry. Is there anything I can do?
Stephanie: No thanks, Mom. I feel better just talking to you.

Conversation Five
Brian: Erica, I found that report we were looking for.
Erica: Great! Let's take a look at it.
Brian: Achoooo!
Erica: Oh, Brian, are you still not feeling well?

Brian: Yeah. This morning I felt better, but now my head hurts.

Erica: Are you getting enough sleep?

Brian: I slept a lot last night, but I still feel tired.

Erica: Listen, Brian. I can handle things here today. Why don't you go home and rest? We can finish this project tomorrow. There's no hurry.

Brian: Thanks, Erica. I might just do that.

Conversation Six

Doug: Jenny, wait up!

Jenny: Doug! I'm glad to see you. I wanted to tell you how much fun I had last weekend.

Doug: Yeah. We enjoyed it too. We always enjoy hiking in the mountains. Unfortunately, Mary and I are both scratching like crazy.

Jenny: Oh no. Poison oak?

Doug: I'm afraid so. We both have a rash on our legs.

Jenny: Oh, Doug. That's too bad.

Doug: Yeah. We feel really itchy.

Jenny: Oh no. We had such a nice day together!

Doug: Yeah. We had a good time, too. Next time we'll be more careful.

Listening 2, page 113:
Giving Advice

Hiro: I'm always sick! What can I do?

Friend: Hiro, you know what you could do? You could drop a class. You're taking too many classes, and you can't do everything. Drop a class, and you'll be able to finish the semester and get better grades.

Hiro: I'm always sick! What should I do?

Mother: Hiro, you should stop eating junk food. I know you're busy, but you always eat hamburgers and pizza and soda. That food is terrible for your health!

Hiro: I'm always sick! What should I do?

Doctor: Mr. Yakumura, you have to stop smoking. Smoking causes many serious diseases, but it also causes many minor illnesses. You get sick very often because you smoke.

Listening 3, page 116:
Making an Appointment

Susan: Hello. Doctor Basso's office. This is Susan. May I help you?

Ms. Kim: Hello. This is So-Young Kim. I'd like to make an appointment with Dr. Basso.

Susan: What seems to be the problem, Ms. Kim?

Ms. Kim: Actually, I'm not sick. I'd like to come in for my yearly checkup.

Susan: OK, fine. Dr. Basso has some time next Thursday. Is that day good for you?

Ms. Kim: Let me see. Thursday. Actually, Thursday isn't good for me. What about the following Tuesday?

Susan: Yes. We have openings on Tuesday. How about Tuesday then?

Ms. Kim: Yeah. Tuesday would be just fine. What time?

Susan: We have an opening at 4:15.

Ms. Kim: 4:15 sounds good.

Susan: OK. Can you spell your name?

Ms. Kim: Kim. K-I-M. First name So-Young. S-O Y-O-U-N-G.

Susan: All right, Ms. Kim. We have you scheduled to come in next Tuesday, March 17 at 4:15. You'll see Dr. Basso for a checkup. Is that correct?

Ms. Kim: Yes. Thank you.

Susan: You're welcome. See you next Tuesday.

Ms. Kim: See you Tuesday.

Listening 4, page 118:
Talking to a Doctor

Part 1

Doctor: Hello, Michelle. I'm Dr. Benson.

Michelle: Hi.

Doctor: How are you feeling today?

Michelle: Not so good.

Doctor: Well, what seems to be the problem?

Michelle: I have a bad cold.

Doctor: I can hear that. How long have you had it?

Michelle: About three weeks. Every time I think it's going away, I get sick again.

Doctor: OK, Michelle. I'm going to examine you now.

Part 2

Doctor: Michelle, we didn't find an infection. That's good. That means that you only have a bad cold. That means that you don't need to take any medicine. But I know that you don't feel very well. I want to ask you some questions, all right?

Michelle: OK.

Doctor: Has school been very difficult lately?

Michelle: Yes. I just finished taking my midterms.

Doctor: Have you been eating well?

Michelle: Well . . . not really. I've been drinking a lot of coffee to stay up late to study.

Doctor: What about exercise? Have you been able to get any exercise during midterm exams?

Michelle: No. I've been studying so much I haven't had time.

Doctor: Well, Michelle. It sounds to me as though you've been studying so much that you haven't given your body a chance to get better. When you're sick, you need to pay attention to your body. I'm going to give you some advice. If you follow my advice, you'll start to feel better soon. OK?

Michelle: OK.

Doctor: Well, first, you must sleep more. You need to get at least seven or eight hours of sleep every night. You cannot study well if you don't get enough sleep.

Michelle: I know.

Doctor: Next, you have to eat better. Your body cannot work well if you don't give it good food. Try to eat more vegetables and fruits. And limit your coffee to two cups a day.

Michelle: OK.

Doctor: Finally, you should exercise more. Try to exercise at least three times per week. It doesn't have to be running or aerobics. Walking is an excellent exercise and is easy to do.

Michelle: All right.

Doctor: Any questions?

Michelle: So you think I should sleep more, eat better, and exercise more. If I do those things, I'll feel better?

Doctor: And you won't get sick as often, Michelle.

Michelle: Thanks a lot, Doctor.

Doctor: You're very welcome, Michelle. Take care.

Listening 5, page 122:
Exercise Information Line

Healthphone Topic 364: Exercise

Most people know that exercise is important. But many people don't exercise. In this announcement you will hear the five most common reasons why people don't exercise. You will also hear some easy solutions.

The first problem? No time. "I don't have any time to exercise. I'm too busy." But you don't need a lot of time to exercise. Short periods of exercise are just as good as long periods of exercise. The solution? You should take two or three short walks every day. For example, ten minutes in the morning, ten min-utes at lunch, and ten minutes after dinner.

Next, money. "I don't have money to go to a gym. I don't have money to buy expensive shoes." No problem. You don't have to spend money to exercise. All you need is a street and comfortable clothes. Our solution? Walk. Don't drive. For instance, walk to the store, to the library, to the bank. Walking is free and easy.

The third most common reason is bad weather. "It's raining. It's too hot. It's snowing." Here's a solution. Exercise inside. For example, turn on some music. Dance. Or clean the house. You can go to the shopping mall and walk fast.

Fourth, people say they're tired. "I'm too tired to exercise. I'll exercise when I have more energy." But exercise gives you energy. Most people feel too tired because they don't exercise. The solution? Exercise every day. Take a walk. Go for a bike ride. Run around the block. You'll feel great! And you won't feel tired.

Finally, some people feel embarrassed. "I feel silly exercising. I don't have a great body." Listen to this solution: Don't feel bad; you should feel great! You're taking care of your body. Little by little, you will feel better. Just do it!

You have heard the five reasons why people don't exercise. More importantly, you have heard five solutions to overcome these problems. Now that you have heard this message, go out and exercise! Good luck.

Listening 6, page 125: Staying Healthy

This lecture will give you advice on how to stay healthy. It will cover ten ways to stay healthy.

First, exercise every day. Exercise will help you to maintain your weight. It will also help you to prevent health problems such as cancer and heart disease. Finally, exercise makes you feel good! So get a little exercise every day.

Second, get enough sleep. Most people don't get enough sleep. But sleep helps you to think clearly and do good work. Your body needs to rest. Then you have energy to do your best. So try to sleep at least seven or eight hours every night.

Third, eat green things. All green food is good for you. For example, spinach, broccoli, green beans, artichokes, kale, cabbage, green apples, and grapes. Fruits and vegetables are very important to your health. So eat some green things today!

Fourth, don't smoke. Smoking causes cancer and other diseases. It can hurt your friends and family when you smoke. It costs a lot of money. So don't smoke.

Fifth, don't drink a lot of alcohol. Alcohol can cause a lot of problems. Many car accidents are caused by alcohol. Alcohol can make you overweight. So drink a little if you like. But don't drink a lot.

Sixth, wear a seat belt. Many people are injured or killed because they aren't wearing a

seat belt. Don't drive with anyone who is not wearing a seat belt. And make sure your passengers are all wearing a seat belt before you drive. Buckle up!

Seventh, drink lots of water. Everyone should drink 6–8 glasses of water every day. Your body needs water to work well. Water also has no calories. People who drink a lot of water don't feel as hungry. So drink up!

Eighth, visit your doctor for regular checkups. During a checkup your doctor can give you tests and check your health. Many serious health problems are found during a regular checkup. So don't go to the doctor only when you are sick. See the doctor once a year for a checkup.

Ninth, reduce stress. Stress causes many serious health problems. It affects your personal and professional lives. Try to have less stress in your life. Relax more! Stress less.

Tenth, spend time with friends and family. We all need to enjoy our life with others. Your friends and family will make you feel good. If you feel good, you will stay healthy! So make time for your loved ones.

The Sound of It, page 126: Pronouncing the /th/ Sound

1. sign

2. thin

3. throat

4. tree

5. tenth

6. mouse

Listening Activity, page 126: Ten Ways to Stay Healthy

You have heard ten ways to stay healthy. We hope you will remember these and follow our advice. First, exercise everyday. Second, get enough sleep. Third, eat green things. Fourth, don't smoke. Fifth, don't drink a lot of alcohol. Sixth, wear a seatbelt. Seventh, drink lots of water. Eighth, visit your doctor for regular checkups. Ninth, reduce stress. Tenth, spend time with friends and family.

CHAPTER 6: A HUMAN RAINBOW

Listening 1, page 135:
Listen for Details

Kim and Angela are good friends. They are a lot alike. In fact, in some ways they are like twins. If you look at the picture, you can see that they are alike in many ways. For example, Kim and Angela are both 20 years old. Right now they are both going to college, but they live at home. Both women live with their parents. They even have similar families. Kim has one brother and one sister, and so does Angela. They both like to listen to rock music, but they don't play all of the time. Angela and Kim both study hard. Both Angela and Kim want to get a good job so that they can move out of their parents' houses. Who knows? Maybe they'll be roommates some day.

Listening 2, page 141: Immigration

The population of American cities grew quickly in the late 1800s. In the early part of the century, most people were farmers. They lived in the country or in small towns. But after 1860, the cities began to grow quickly. In 1860 there was only one city, New York City, that had over 500,000 people in the United States. Only 40 years later, there were seven very large cities and many smaller ones.

One of the reasons why the cities grew so quickly was because of the large numbers of immigrants. Many immigrants adapted to life in the United States by going to parts of the cities where there were people from their own country. In cities across America, Italians lived in Little Italy. Poles settled in Little Warsaw. Many cities had a Chinatown. Cities like Chicago and New York had neighborhoods of Italians, Irish, Polish, Hungarian, German, Jewish, and Chinese people. In their neighborhoods, the immigrants spoke their own languages, celebrated their own holidays, and ate their native foods.

Language Learning Strategy,
page 141: Invent a Title

1. Maria is from French Guiana, in South America. Last year she immigrated to Montreal, Canada, to live with her sister. Maria chose to move to Montreal to be with her sister and because the people in Montreal speak French like the people in French Guiana. She thought it would be easier to immigrate to a new country if she already knew the language. Although the French in French Guiana is a little different than the French in Montreal, Maria found it easy to adapt to the language.

   The weather was a little more difficult for Maria. French Guiana is a warm country. Maria had never seen snow before she went to Montreal. The snow looked very beautiful falling down from the sky. But when Maria went outside, she was surprised how cold it was. Maria had to buy a warm winter coat.

2. Michael was born in the United States; however, his mother is an immigrant. Michael is a mixture of different races. His mother is Cuban and Puerto Rican, and his father is African American. When he is at home, Michael speaks Spanish with his mother and grandmother. He speaks English with his father and when he's at college. Michael is lucky to be bilingual. He is especially lucky because he learned both languages as a child. He doesn't have an accent in Spanish or English.

3. Rachel lives in Ohio. She is a typical American teenager. Like most Americans, Rachel's ancestors immigrated to the United States. Actually, she is a mixture of several different backgrounds. She is Irish, Swedish, English, German, and several other nationalities. Even though Rachel's ancestors come from several different nationalities, she doesn't know any language except English. Her family has been living in the United States for several generations. Rachel is interested in how her ancestors came to the United States. This summer she is going to help her grandmother research her family background.

4. Billy lives near Tuba City, Arizona. Billy is a Native American. He is from the Navajo tribe. His ancestors lived in the desert many years before Europeans came to North America. Billy goes to school and works on his father's ranch. He helps his father raise horses. He also has a horse of his own. Billy's favorite thing to do in the summer is to go to the Indian Rodeo. Billy speaks Navajo at home with his family; at school he uses both Navajo and English.

CHAPTER 7: MY HERO

Listening 1, page 161: Heroes

Florence Griffith Joyner

Almost everyone knew Florence Griffith Joyner as Flojo. Flojo was one of the world's best female runners. She was especially good at running short races. She won medals at two different Olympic games. She won a silver medal in the 200-meter sprint at the 1984 Olympics. She won four Olympic medals, three gold and one silver, in the 1988 Olympics. In 1988 she was female athlete of the year.

Flojo grew up in Los Angeles. She came from a large family. She was the seventh of eleven children.

She was more than just a powerful athlete— she was also a fashion model, clothes designer, and an intelligent person. In her spare time, she wrote poetry. She was also a role model for young female athletes. She showed them that female athletes could be strong and beautiful too. When young girls told her she was their role model, Flojo would say: "Don't be like me. Be better than me."

She used her fame as an athlete to help many people. She raised money for charities like the American Cancer Society, and she created the Florence Griffith Joyner Youth Foundation to help poor children. In 1993, she became the chair of the President's Council on Physical Fitness.

Unfortunately, Flojo died of a heart defect in 1998. President Bill Clinton said this about Flojo: "America and the world has lost one of our greatest Olympians. We were dazzled by her speed, humbled by her talent, and captivated by her style. Though she rose to the highest place in the world of sports yet, she never forgot where she came from."

Bob Marley

Bob Marley was from Jamaica. He grew up very poor. His father was an English sea captain, and his mother was a poor woman from Jamaica. Bob's mother used to sing to him when he was a child. He grew up loving music. He played guitar and sang a special kind of music called reggae. Reggae music uses the traditional rhythms from African music. But Bob Marley did more than sing. His song had a message. He sang songs about the poverty of the people in Jamaica. He sang songs about racism and injustice. One of his most famous songs is "Get Up Stand Up." Today Bob Marley's music is known almost everywhere around the world. Bob Marley died of cancer in 1981, but his music still lives in the hearts of many people.

Celine Dion

Celine Dion has always loved to sing, and she is good at it too. Her voice has been familiar to the people in her native land of Quebec for a long time. But she was not so well known internationally, because she sang primarily in French. She began to get wider attention in 1982 when she won an international singing award in Japan. A year later she was the first Canadian to have a best-selling record in France. Because Celine sang in French, she was not well-known outside of France and Canada. She became an international superstar when she began singing in English. You may know some of her English songs, such as "Because You Loved Me" and "My Heart Will Go On."

Celine is admired not only for her voice, but also for her caring personality. She has used her star power and musical gifts to benefit the Canadian Cystic Fibrosis Foundation. Cystic fibrosis is a disease that is inherited by children from their parents. As of now, there is no cure for cystic fibrosis. Celine hopes that she will be able to call attention to the disease so that scientists can find a cure for the disease in the future.

Sammy Sosa

Sammy Sosa is a hero not just because he hits lots of home runs, and not just because he was voted the Most Valuable Player in the National Baseball League in 1998; he is a hero because he remembers his family and the people of the Dominican Republic, where he came from. Sammy's father died when he was seven years old. When he was very young, he sold oranges and shined shoes in order to help his mother and his five brothers and sisters. There were many times when his family just didn't have enough to eat.

When he was older, Sammy came to the United States to play baseball.

Today, Sammy is a hero in the Dominican Republic. He gives thousands of dollars to hospitals, charities, and hurricane relief for the people of the Dominican Republic. He also built a shopping center just for the poor people in his own neighborhood in the Dominican Republic.

For Sammy, the most important thing is his family. Today he lives with his wife and four children and his brother Juan in Chicago. He is happiest when he is at home playing with his children. In the Dominican Republic, Sammy bought his mother two houses. Every time he hits a home run he thinks of his mother. He blows her a kiss.

Hillary Rodham Clinton

You may recognize this woman as the wife of William Jefferson Clinton, but Hillary Rodham Clinton is more than just a first lady. She is a hero to many women. She is a very intelligent lawyer. Also, she is active in making changes that make life better for all people, but especially children. When her husband first ran for president of the United States in 1992, Hillary became a powerful symbol of the changing role and status of women in American society.

After graduating from Yale Law School, Hillary went to work for the Children's Defense Fund, an organization that lobbies for children's welfare. This was the beginning of her career as a defender of the rights of children. In 1977, she started Arkansas Advocates for Children and Families. She also worked with her husband to try to reform health care in the United States. In 1996 she published a book about children, *It Takes a Village*. This book shows how all people must work together to take care of the children in a community.

Listening 2, page 165: Superman

He isn't real, but he is one hero that everyone recognizes. He's tall and strong. He has broad shoulders and dark hair. He wears blue tights and a red cape. His suit has a big "S" on it. He can fly. He can see through walls. He can bend a steel rod. Bul-

lets can't hurt him. He fights for good, and he always gets the bad guys. He's Superman.

When he isn't flying around catching bad guys, Superman is Clark Kent. Clark Kent is a quiet man. He's a newspaper reporter. Clark Kent isn't flashy like Superman. He doesn't wear blue tights. He wears a business suit and glasses. Even though Clark Kent is also tall and strong, no one notices that he is really Superman.

Lois Lane is a reporter too. She is intelligent and beautiful. She is a good reporter. She does almost anything to get a story for her newspaper, *The Daily Planet*. She's always getting into trouble with bad guys. Superman has to rescue her. Lois works with Clark Kent, but she doesn't notice that Clark Kent and Superman are the same person.

Listening 3, page 173: Personal Heroes

Kate: I was watching this interesting news story on TV last night. It was about how important it is for children and especially teenagers to have heroes. One of the things they said is that children who admire someone are more well adjusted than children who don't have heroes. It got me thinking about heroes, you know what I mean? Well, of course I think my parents are good role models. They are like heroes to me because they really care about me. But I was thinking, who else would I consider as a hero? What about you guys? Do you have a hero? Who's your hero, Robert?

Robert: Well, I have to say that my hero is Martin Luther King. I mean, he was a person that really made a difference with his life. He stood up for the rights of all people. He fought hard against racism and discrimination, but he did it in a peaceful way. That takes guts. He fought for what he believed in even though it seemed like everyone was against him. He even died fighting racism. He was really a good person. African Americans owe a lot to him. He was really brave.

Nancy: You're right, Dr. King was a good role model for all people African American, Whites, and Navajos, like me. But I think we all choose heroes who are like us in some way. I mean someone we can be proud of because they come from the same background that we do.

Kate: Are there Native American heroes?

Nancy: Yeah. Have you ever heard of the Navajo code-talkers?

Robert: Code-talkers?

Nancy: Yeah. During World War II, the U.S. was having problems keeping military secrets because the enemy kept on breaking our secret codes. They'd figure out what we were going to do or where the soldiers were and stuff like that. Do you know how they finally managed to fool them?

Kate: How?

Nancy: They got Navajos to send and receive messages on the radio. They spoke in their Navajo language. The enemy never figured out what the code was, because they couldn't speak Navajo. The code-talkers were very brave. They had to be at the most dangerous places in the battle to send and receive messages. They made a really important contribution to the war. All Native Americans know about code-talkers and consider them heroes. Not just because they were brave, but also because they were Navajos using the Navajo language. They are real role models for the younger generation.

Kate: That's a great story. I see why Navajos consider them as heroes.

Robert: OK, so who's your hero, Kate?

Kate: Well, I guess that Mother Teresa of Calcutta would have to be a hero for me. I admire her a lot because she really worked hard to help people who couldn't really help themselves—the really poor people. She lived and worked with the very poorest people in Calcutta, India. She helped feed them and take care of them when they were sick. She talked about their problems and got other people to help them out. Did you know that she won the Nobel Peace Prize?

Robert: Yeah, Martin Luther King won the Peace Prize, too.

Nancy: I think we're pretty well adjusted. We have great heroes to be our role models.
(They all laugh.)

Robert: Yeah, I guess you're right.

CHAPTER 8: GET A JOB

Listening 1, page 185:
Talking About Work

1. Felix is a receptionist. He works in an office. All day he answers the phone and types memos and letters. He also phones people for his boss. He makes appointments for people who want to see his boss. Felix likes his job because he doesn't take work home. He finishes work at 5:00 every evening, and then he goes home.

2. Claudia is a firefighter. Sometimes she works nights, and sometimes she works during the day. When she works at night, she sleeps at the fire station. Claudia fights fires. Claudia works hard to stay in shape. She must be in good shape to put out fires. So every day she jogs and lifts weights. Firefighting is heavy work. Claudia likes her work because it is an important job. She saves lives. Claudia also knows how to help people who are injured.

3. Bernice is a server. She works at a busy restaurant. She takes people's orders and serves them food. She also takes people's money and gives them change. When the restaurant is really busy, sometimes she evens cooks the food. She works six days a week. Her job is not easy. The trays of food are heavy. She always gets backaches from carrying the heavy trays. Besides that, she has to be on her feet all day. Often her feet get tired. Bernice doesn't really like her job, but she has to work because she needs the money. She hopes she can find a better job soon.

The Sound of It, page 188:
Three Different Ways to Say *s*

works	lives	teaches	helps	cooks	washes
makes	buys	sells	phones	keeps	fixes
drives	watches	does	builds	delivers	treats
prices	thinks	repairs	sees	takes	reads

Listening 2, page 195:
A Career Plan

Here are some easy steps to follow to plan your career. If you follow these steps, you will be successful. First, you should do a self-assessment. A self-assessment is a way to find out about yourself. A self-assessment helps you find out about your interests, skills, and personality. You can do this by taking a formal survey, or by writing down the things you like to do and the things you are good at. Second, you should gather information about different occupations. There are many books and magazines that tell about different jobs. Find these books and study them. Who knows? You may find out about a job that you did not know existed. You should also talk to people about different kinds of jobs. Talk to people who are doing the job you are interested in, or talk to your teacher or counselor at school. The books and people can help you find out two important things: how much time it will take to study for your career and what is the best way to get the education and training you need. This will also help you decide if you have the time and the money to reach your career goal. The third thing you have to do is to get the skills you need. You can do this by getting more education at a college, university, or technical school or by learning on the job. The final step is to learn how to find a job. Once you finish your training, you cannot sit and wait for jobs to come to you. You must show what you know in a job interview. You also need to present yourself in a résumé.

CHAPTER 9: ALL IN THE FAMILY

Listening 1, page 215:
Talking About Family

Part 1

Juan: Makiko, tell me about your family.

Makiko: Sure. It won't take very long! My family is pretty small.

Juan: Really? How many people are in your family?

Makiko: There are just five of us. My parents, my sister, and my grandmother.

Juan: Is your sister older or younger than you?

Makiko: She's older than me, and she never lets me forget it!

Juan: Does your grandmother live with you?

Makiko: Yes, she does. It's wonderful having her with us.

Part 2

Makiko: What about your family, Juan? Is your family big or small?

Juan: My family is pretty big. There are my parents, my grandparents, and my brothers and sisters. I have three brothers and two sisters.

Makiko: Wow! Are you the oldest or the youngest?

Juan: Actually, I'm in the middle.

Makiko: Do all your grandparents live with you?

Juan: No, but they're here all the time. My grandparents live nearby, with my uncle.

Makiko: So how many people are there in your family?

Juan: Well, without counting cousins and aunts and uncles, there are eleven people in my family.

Listening 2, page 217:
Talking About Pets

Part 1

Speaker One: Do you have a pet?

Speaker Two: Yes! I have a cat named Emma.

Speaker One: Emma! What a pretty name. Tell me about her.

Speaker Two: Well, she's two years old, she's very sweet, and she's very loving.

Speaker One: Oh, I'm sure she is. Cats are so affectionate. Do you have a picture?

Speaker Two: I'm embarrassed to say that I do have a picture. Here she is.

Speaker One: Oh. How pretty. Is she really two years old? She's so small.

Speaker Two: Yeah. She just turned two last month. She's stopped growing. I guess she's just a little cat!

Speaker One: She looks playful in this picture. Is she?

Speaker Two: She's really playful. She loves to chase string and climb inside paper bags and boxes. In fact, I wish I had more time to play with her. She'd like to play all day!

Speaker One: I'd love to meet her someday.

Part 2

Speaker Two: What about you? Do you have a pet?

Speaker One: Yes. I have a dog named Luce.

Speaker Two: Do you have a picture of Luce?

Speaker One: No, but I can tell you about her. She's very big, with short golden hair. And she's really friendly.

Speaker Two: I guess a big dog eats a lot of food.

Speaker One: Oh my gosh! She eats so much food! I have to buy it in these huge bags!

Speaker Two: Oh no! What do you do together?

Speaker One: Luce loves to go to the park to see other dogs. She likes to play with them. Actually, she wants to play with cats, too. But the cats don't want to play with her!

Speaker Two: I guess Emma and Luce wouldn't like each other.

Speaker One: Probably not!

Listening 3, page 218:
Pet Statistics

Today I will tell you some interesting facts about pets in the United States and in Canada. First of all, does anyone know how many households in the United States and Canada have pets? If you said 60%, you're right! Sixty percent of households have at least one pet.

What about the most popular pets? Does anyone know what the most popular pet is? Dogs are very popular. In fact, dogs and cats are the two most popular types of pets. Other popular pets are birds and fish. Some people have dogs and cats *and* birds and fish!

Now let's talk about how pets help their owners. You probably know that people help their pets. They feed them and take care of them. But did you know that pets help their owners? Pets help their owners to feel good. People who don't have pets often feel lonely, especially older people. Pets can also help people's health. It's true! People with pets are healthier than people without pets.

OK. Finally, I'll tell you that people in the United States and Canada love their pets like members of their own family. Many people let their pets sleep in their beds. And sometimes pet owners carry a picture of their pet with them!

I hope you learned something today about pets in the United States and Canada. Any questions?

Listening 4, page 223:
How People Meet

First Story

My husband and I met in high school. During our senior year, we studied biology together. We talked and laughed a lot during class. One Friday, we joked that we should go on a date that night. At first, I didn't know if he was serious. He didn't know if I was joking. That night I put on a new dress and waited. He had a more difficult time. He had to knock on the door without knowing if I would be ready or not. But he knocked, and I was ready! That was our first date. This year, we celebrated our fortieth wedding anniversary!

Second Story

My husband and I met one day at an airport. It was Christmas day. I was picking up my friend Bernd. He was coming from Germany to spend the holidays with my family. While we were waiting for his luggage, I heard a man speaking in Italian. I decided to say something to him because I speak Italian. I said, "Buon Natale" which means, "Merry Christmas!" When I spoke in Italian, he said, "Mama mia! Why do you speak Italian? Who are you?" He asked me for my phone number. He called me the next day, and we dated for a year. Then we got married. So be careful who you talk to in the airport!

Third Story

My wife and I met through our parents. Our parents arranged our marriage. Before we got married, my wife and I wanted to meet. Our parents arranged our first meeting in a restaurant. That night, we talked about ourselves and what we wanted in our lives. We talked for hours. We shared our hopes and dreams. After a while, we decided that our parents were right! And we got married.

Fourth Story

My wife and I met through a matchmaker. I'm an engineer, and in my field, most people are men. I couldn't meet any women at work. So one day I saw an advertisement for a matchmaking service, and I decided to call. The matchmaker introduced me to many nice women. I enjoyed meeting them, but I didn't meet anyone I wanted to marry. Finally, she introduced me to my wife. I decided not to date any other women because I liked her very much. We enjoyed the same things, and we laughed a lot together. We also had the same goals and values in life. My wife and I were married six years ago, and now we have two children. I'm glad I picked up the phone and called that matchmaker!

The Sound of It, page 226:
The Simple Past /-ed/Sound

1. We study biology in the same class.

2. He knocked on the door.

3. He asked me for my phone number.

4. We talk about our lives.

5. I decided to call.

We *talked* and *laughed* a lot during class.
I *answered* the door.
We *dated* for a year.

1. Celebrate. Celebrated. We celebrated our fortieth wedding anniversary this year.

2. Call. Called. He called me the next day.

3. Arrange. Arranged. Our parents arranged our marriage.

4. Want. Wanted. My wife and I wanted to meet.

5. Like. Liked. I liked her very much.

CHAPTER 10: THE FUTURE IS NOW

Listening 1, page 235:
Toys of the Future

Amazing Amy is the doll of the future. Amy will be an interactive doll. She will talk to children. She will be able to say more than 10,000 phrases. But she's not just another talking doll. Amy will have special food and a bottle. She will react to the child who plays with her. When a child feeds her, she will be happy. She will also react when the child changes her clothes. Amy will wake up when the child wakes up. She will act tired when it is time for the child to go to bed. Children will have fun playing with Amy.

Toy trucks have been favorite toys for a long time. Chuck, My Talkin' Truck, will be the toy of the future for kids ages two and up. Chuck will be a dump truck that comes to life. Children will say his name, and Chuck will talk back. He will say things like "Let's get rolling!" and "Great job, let's get another load!" Besides that, he will make other "truck" noises.

Lego building blocks have been a favorite toy for decades. Now Legos will be a high-tech toy.

Soon, children will be able to make Robots with the Lego Mindstorms system. The robots will have sensors. The sensors will respond to light and touch. The sensors will get information from the environment. The sensors will turn on motors. The children will program their robots to do different things. But the best part is that Lego Mindstorms will be like traditional Legos. Children will be able to use the toys again and again. They will be able to build robots that play sports. These robots can shoot baskets and play hockey. Children will be able to build as many robots as their imagination allows.

When is the best time to learn a new language? Everyone knows it is when you are a child. In fact, researchers have found that it is easiest to learn a second language between ages one and five. With this toy, Little Linguist, learning a new language will be like a game for young children. Little Linguist will be a multisensory experience. Children will be able to see, hear, and touch things from everyday life as they learn new words. It will be an interactive toy. It will allow children to learn a second language the way they learned their first language. They will be able to learn English, Spanish, and French. When they use Little Linguist, children will hear a word and associate it with a familiar object. Finally, they will begin to use the word in simple sentences.

Language Learning Strategy, page 242: Use Pictures and Photos

Most people use cars to go short distances. They drive to work, school, or to the grocery story or the mall. Most people don't need cars that drive hundreds of miles every day. That's why some people believe that cars in the future will be powered by electricity, natural gas, or other fuels besides gasoline. Here are some Most people use cars to go short distances. They drive to work, school, or to the grocery story or the mall. Most people don't need cars that drive hundreds of miles every day. That's why some people believe that cars in the future will be powered by electricity, natural gas, or other fuels besides gasoline. Here are some examples of cars you are going to see on the streets in the future.

1. The electric Lotus Elise is an electric sports car. It has two electric engines. It can go 120 miles before it needs to be recharged. The engines are very powerful, but they are lightweight. The motors only weigh about 40 pounds each. The Lotus Elise is among the fastest of electric cars. It can go 90 miles per hour. However, it is a small car. It can only carry (pause). It can only carry two passengers.

2. The City Bee is a perfect car for the city. It was created in Norway. It is small, yet roomy and safe. It can hold two passengers. It is designed to be easy to take care of. So the repair bills will be low. The electric City Bee doesn't pollute. What's more, it is totally recyclable. The City Bee can go about 70 miles before it needs to be recharged. You can even drive it on the freeway. It can go (pause). It can go 65 miles per hour.

3. The Sunrise is a family car. It can hold four people. The Sunrise is a strong but lightweight electric car. That makes it safe, but it also goes a long way on every electric charge. Like the City Bee, the Sunrise can go 65 miles per hour. However, the Sunrise has a big advantage over other electric cars. It has set a record for driving the longest distance without being recharged. The Sunrise went 373 miles on a single electric charge. The Sunrise was created in the United States. It is not for sale yet, but (pause). It is not for sale yet, but it will be available soon.

SKILLS INDEX

LISTENING & SPEAKING SKILLS

Jorge's Schedule

	SUN	MON	TUES	WED	THUR	FRI	SAT
MORNING	read the newspaper	work	work	work	work	work	sleep in late
AFTERNOON	relax	class	class	class	class	study	play soccer
EVENING	study	study	work out at the gym	study	work out at the gym	relax	go to the movies

Makito's Schedule

	SUN	MON	TUES	WED	THUR	FRI	SAT
M O R N I N G	study	work	work	work	work	work	study
A F T E R N O O N	study	work	work	work	work	work	study
E V E N I N G	watch TV	class	class	class	class	go out with friends	stay home

From the train depot you want to take Santa Cruz Ave. toward El Camino Real. Follow Santa Cruz Ave. for about a half mile. You'll pass many stores and a bank on the left. Take a left on University Drive. Go four blocks on University until you get to Middle Ave. Take a left onto Middle. The park is on your left.

From Nealon Park, take Middle Ave. toward El Camino Real. Turn left onto El Camino and go three blocks. Take a right at Ravenswood. You'll know it because you'll see a big bookstore on the corner of Ravenswood and El Camino. Take the first right past the railroad tracks. That's Alma. The library is on Alma, on your left.

TEXT CREDITS

pp. 17–18: Adapted from *Hands Around the World: 365 Creative Ways to Build Cultural Awareness and Global Respect.* Copyright 1992 by Susan Milord. Williamson Publishing Co.

pp. 28–30: Adapted from "Use Public Transportation." Copyright 1992 by Susan Milord. Williamson Publishing Co.

p. 221: "Brave Hearts" by Dan Jewel and Sopheronia Scott Gregory © People Weekly 1997.

ART CREDITS

pp. 36–37: Reprinted with permission from West Valley College.

p. 69: Reprinted with permission from Moviefone.

p. 118: Reprinted with permission from San Jose State University Health Center.

p. 224: Reprinted with permission from Mile High Adventures.

PHOTO CREDITS

p. iv: T, TM, M, BM Photographs by Jonathan Stark for the Heinle & Heinle Image Resource Bank; B Jack Hollingsworth/CORBIS. p. vi: T & BM Photographs by Jonathan Stark for the Heinle & Heinle Image Resource Bank; TM Bettmann/CORBIS; M Jim Zuckerman/CORBIS. p. 2: Photograph by Jonathan Stark for the Heinle & Heinle Image Resource Bank. p. 8: The Purcell Team/CORBIS. p. 17: AFP/CORBIS. p. 20: TR Michael Newman/PhotoEdit; BL Ronnen Eshel/CORBIS; BR Steve Skjold/PhotoEdit; OTHERS Photographs by Jonathan Stark for the Heinle & Heinle Image Resource Bank. p. 26: TL Jose Carillo/PhotoEdit; TR Owen Franken/CORBIS; B Photograph by Jonathan Stark for the Heinle & Heinle Image Resource Bank. p. 28: Bob Krist//CORBIS. p. 29: T Kevin R. Morris/CORBIS; B Daniel Laine/CORBIS. p. 30: Craig Lovell/CORBIS. p. 57: T Photograph by Jonathan Stark for the Heinle & Heinle Image Resource Bank; B Laura Dwight/CORBIS. p. 58: Bob Rowan, Progressive Image/CORBIS. p. 69: Bettmann/CORBIS. p. 78: Photograph by Jonathan Stark for the Heinle & Heinle Image Resource Bank. p. 80: TL Scott T. Smith/CORBIS; TR Paul A. Souders/CORBIS; BL Annie Griffiths Belt/CORBIS; BR Jim Richardson/ CORBIS. p. 81: T Spencer Grant/PhotoEdit; B Photograph by Jonathan Stark for the Heinle & Heinle Image Resource Bank. p. 82: W. Perry Conway/CORBIS. p. 84: Dave Bartruff/CORBIS. p. 87: Wolfgang Kaehler/CORBIS. p. 89: Robert Pickett/CORBIS. p. 97: Photograph by Jonathan Stark for the Heinle & Heinle Image Resource Bank. p. 105: Jack Hollingsworth/CORBIS. p. 109: TL CORBIS; M Steve Raymer/CORBIS; BL Robert Holmes/CORBIS; BR Tony Arruza/CORBIS. p. 110: CORBIS. pp. 113–135: Photographs by Jonathan Stark for the Heinle & Heinle Image Resource Bank. p. 138: Bettmann/CORBIS. p. 140: Robert Brenner/PhotoEdit. p. 141: T Photograph by Jonathan Stark for the Heinle & Heinle Image Resource Bank: B Joseph Sohm: ChromoSohm Inc./CORBIS. p. 145: Bettman/CORBIS. p. 147: Charles E. Rotkin/CORBIS. p. 157: T Bettman/CORBIS; BL AFP/CORBIS; BR Flip Schulke/CORBIS. p. 158: Craig Lovell/CORBIS p. 159: TR Wally McNamee/CORBIS; TL AFP/CORBIS; TM S.I.N./CORBIS; BR AFP/CORBIS; BL David Allen/CORBIS. p. 162: TL & TM AFP/CORBIS; TR Bettman/CORBIS; MR Flip Schulke/CORBIS; ML S.I.N./CORBIS; BL David Allen/CORBIS; BM AFP/CORBIS; BR Wally McNamee/CORBIS. p. 164: Bettman/CORBIS. p. 172: Flip Schulke/CORBIS. p. 177: Photograph by Jonathan Stark for the Heinle & Heinle Image Resource Bank. p. 178: Bettmann/CORBIS. p. 180: Photographs by Jonathan Stark for the Heinle & Heinle Image Resource Bank. p. 183: T & B Photographs by Jonathan Stark for the Heinle & Heinle Image Resource Bank; M Jim Zuckerman/CORBIS. p. 184: T Reuters Dateline/Archive Photos; B Mitchell Gerber/CORBIS. p. 185: T & B AFP/CORBIS; TM Ronnen Eshel/CORBIS; BM Mitchell Gerber/CORBIS. p. 186: T Owen Franken/CORBIS; B Gary Nolan/CORBIS. p. 201: Jaques M. Chenet/CORBIS. p. 204: Photographs by Jonathan Stark for the Heinle & Heinle Image Resource Bank. p. 205: T & TM Photographs by Jonathan Stark for the Heinle & Heinle Image Resource Bank; BM CORBIS; B Jaques M. Chenet/CORBIS. p. 210: Photograph by Jonathan Stark for the Heinle & Heinle Image Resource Bank. p. 210: Photographs by Jonathan Stark for the Heinle & Heinle Image Resource Bank. p. 217: Photographs by Richard Dworak. p. 218: Photograph by Richard Dworak.